Weird Museums

WEIRD MUSEUMS

Published by AA Media Limited, whose registered office is
Grove House, Lutyens Close, Basingstoke, Hampshire RG24 8AG;
registered number 06112600

First published in 2019

A CIP catalogue record for this book is available from the British Library.

ISBN: 978-0-7495-8185-5

Text by Jackie Bates

Publisher: Phil Carroll
Editor: Donna Wood
Art Director: James Tims
Designer: Tracey Freestone

Printed and bound in the UK by Bell & Bain Ltd

A05657

theAA.com

Contents

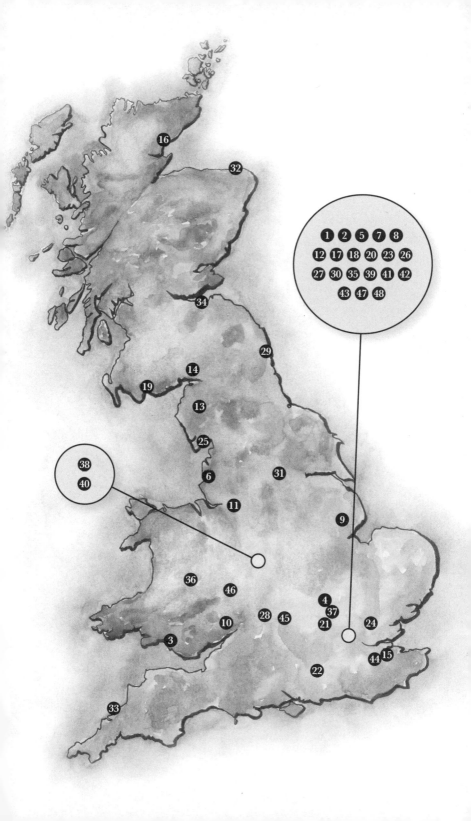

Foreword
by Danny Baker

The magnificent establishments you are about to discover do you the great courtesy of being specific.

While the British Museum may house some of the most interesting items salvaged from the ages, I've found I spend most of my time there consulting a floorplan while trying to convince the attendants I actually meant to walk through the Etruscan vases six times through different doorways.

This is because – and I know this is not a popular opinion – most museums are simply too big. Many years ago, when I went to the Natural History Museum with my young son, we had to eventually ask someone where the Blue Whale skeleton was. Think about that. We couldn't locate a whale in a building with a roof. The maverick souls who created and curate the collections in this mysterious publication offer no such confusion. Nobody will walk into the Antique Breadboard Museum (see page 21) and have to ask where the antique breadboards are. Frankly, if you like antique breadboards the place is like Disney World.

Small though many of the exhibitions in these pages may be, we can give thanks that when wonderful things become miniaturised it doesn't diminish their wonder. That they exist at all is part of their fascination. I have visited the Van Gogh Museum in Amsterdam and made all the right noises as we mooched about it, yet whenever Amsterdam gets mentioned to me I do not think of the master's *Wheatfield with Crows* but rather the Flute of Shame that I saw in the Museum of Historical Torture 10 minutes up the road.

True, you do feel a bit hangdog buying a ticket for a torture museum, but it's not all racks and thumbscrews. The Flute of Shame is a ludicrous metal clarinet that bad musicians were forced to display, via a sort of dog collar, in the 15th century. In an ideal world this astounding exhibit would continually play Don McLean's *Vincent*, thus reminding visitors to the city of their possible next stop. That said, a Torture Museum is probably too mainstream to qualify for this book.

I am certainly not alone in my demand to be mesmerised by the mundane. Over my years on the radio one of the most reliable phone-in subjects has proved to be Odd Tourist Attractions That Listeners Have Attended and it was through this appeal that I first got to know of the Mexican Fleas of Tring (see page 170). That the unassuming borough of Tring had a Natural History Museum at all was startling enough, but to learn that it contained a cabinet wherein fleas were dressed in minute human clothing – the apogee of this skill being a full Mariachi Band – had me legging it to the relevant mainline station. Tring, having been made aware of the Elgin Marbles, had decided to fight back in style and as far as I was concerned had triumphed (see page 170).

Similarly you can keep the Rock & Roll Hall of Fame with its extravagant props, stage outfits and gold discs. I know someone who has a cigarette butt discarded by David Bowie on Victoria station in 1976. He keeps it on a little blue silk cushion and will occasionally wheel it out to silence doubters. And, yes, he calls it his Diamond Dog End.

The point is, delight is in the detail, awe found in shadows. May this book be the torch that illuminates those paths away from the overcrowded tourist highways and brings you into a world of secret ice-wells, ancient mechanical music and Teapot Islands.

'An incoherent vision of the world displayed through wonder,' is the phrase that caught my eye while reading this important work.

I am now off to visit the Anaesthesia Museum (see page 15). I do so hope the first exhibit is a giant mallet. Because, unlike the Metropolitan in New York, once you enter these places you never really know what you're going to find…

Anaesthesia Museum

London

The Anaesthesia Museum is very small, and only open on weekdays. Even then, it's sometimes unexpectedly closed; they recommend that you phone in advance to make an appointment.

The museum is in the basement of the Association of Anaesthetists, so you get to go down the area steps of one of those big fancy West End houses. And as it's just round the corner from BBC Broadcasting House and Harley Street, there are plenty of fine buildings to admire, and the British Dental Museum (see page 36) and Pollock's Toy Museum (see page 188) are both within walking distance.

Anaesthesia became a bit of a theme during the writing of this book. It pops up – not unexpectedly – at the Dental Museum and the Old Operating Theatre Museum (see page 179), and also at the Freud Museum (see page 91). Life being what it is, the search for effective pain relief has been a perennial thread in the human story. Imagining existence without paracetamol is bad enough, but the idea of childbirth, amputation or dental work without anaesthetics is unpleasant to say the least.

One of the most fascinating things about the history of anaesthetics is what happened after the properties of nitrous oxide were discovered (in 1772, by Joseph Priestley, the year after he discovered oxygen). It was to be a long and complicated journey from here to the establishment of its use during operations. Humphry Davy (he of the Davy miners' lamp) noticed that it 'appears capable of destroying physical pain' (he also dubbed it 'laughing gas' apparently) and suggested it could be used as pain relief during surgery as early as 1800, but no dice. One of the reasons for this was the bad reputation the gas acquired due to its use recreationally by poets and other such debauched members of society. This is a theme, in fact; almost every type of anaesthetic was discovered some considerable time before anyone used it as pain relief. Ether was discovered in the 14th century, but anyone requiring the amputation of a gangrenous limb or the extraction of a rotten tooth carried on being given booze or a bang on the head. So be grateful that you live in more enlightened times.

No one wants their patients thrashing about or shrieking when they're trying to operate on them, so for as long as people have needed medical intervention (which is forever) there have been attempts to alleviate their discomfort or render them unconscious. Pressing firmly on the carotid artery or getting them off their faces with alcohol or drugs can be reasonably effective, but it's a bit hit and miss. Come the Enlightenment, everything got a bit more scientific.

It does seem quite bewildering that even though experimentation demonstrated the effectiveness of various gases as anaesthetics, no one seemed to think the time was right to extrapolate from this. It's suggested that the very idea of pain-free surgery was a concept so wildly unlikely that no one could get their heads round it. It's clear from the information in the museum that the reasons for this are as much a mystery to the historians of the subject as to anyone else. It seems that the one person who actively sought to promote inhalation anaesthesia, Henry Hill Hickman, was essentially ignored, and he died young, while laughing gas parties and 'ether frolics' were still popular for kicks.

In contrast to the size of the museum, the history of the subject is vast and complex, with endless twists and turns – but it's described clearly here and you'll certainly feel like you've learned a lot of things you didn't know before, whatever your personal experience of anaesthetics has been. From nitrous oxide demonstrations by American travelling showmen to the removal of a tumour from an anaesthetised patient in front of an audience, progress in the mid-19th century was not entirely smooth, but once news of recent events in the US arrived in Britain in late 1846 things began to speed up.

The gas was used by Robert Liston, London's leading surgeon, for an amputation on 21 December, the first public demonstration in Britain. (Public demonstrations of surgery were once all the rage.) James 'Young' Simpson, Professor of Midwifery in Edinburgh, was in London at the time and instantly saw its potential for improving the experience of childbirth. He also discovered the anaesthetic properties of chloroform in 1847. There were still problems, however – both medical and religious objections, and the occasional death. No one really understood why anaesthesia worked, or how much gas should be administered; there were no particular notions of safe practice; and the administration of the gas was often delegated to more junior members of the team – it wasn't yet a specialism. Dr John Snow became an early expert and published on the subject; it was he who administered chloroform to Queen Victoria for the births of Prince Leopold in 1853 and Princess Beatrice in 1857. After this, of course, everyone pretty much shut up about their objections to the practice. There were continued improvements, including monitoring the patient while unconscious, and more effective drugs and combinations of drugs. Nitrous oxide, for example, was too dangerous for surgery but perfect for tooth extraction (as you'll remember from that scene in *Little Shop of Horrors*…). It had to be manufactured on-site, however, until advances in technology allowed it to be transported under pressure. A lot of different elements had to come together.

Anaesthesia doesn't just cover 'going under' – the museum also explores local anaesthetics, from cooling with sprays of ether to the numbing effects of cocaine. Sigmund Freud studied this in the 1880s, and you can find out more about that at his house in Hampstead (see page 91). Cocaine was effective for eye surgery, and the notion of 'peripheral nerve block' was immediately popular with the medical profession. Further developments in anatomical knowledge eventually resulted in spinal anaesthesia (1898) and the epidural block (1921).

Interwoven with the story of anaesthetics is that of antiseptics. Although anaesthetics meant that longer and more complex surgery could be undertaken, people still died from infection. The improvement in one drove improvements in the other. The horrific injuries suffered by both servicemen and civilians during two world wars also advanced the technology.

Other methods explored and explained at the museum include the use of the South American 'arrow poison', curare, which produces relaxation of the muscles in a way that is especially useful for abdominal surgery. The use of curare means that less anaesthetic is required for this kind of surgery, making it much safer. (If you're a reader of detective fiction, it's interesting to note that each development in the science of anaesthesia was clearly grasped by writers as a useful addition to their murderous repertoire – many of us will have been exposed to chloroform or curare only within the pages of a book.)

By 1950 all the elements of modern anaesthesia were pretty much in place. Although there have been lots of developments in the drugs used, they are very much improvements on a theme rather than new discoveries. Further improvements in training (anaesthetists now undergo nine years of training) and equipment (disposable syringes, computers to control drug levels) mean that these days the practice of anaesthetics is remarkably safe.

Methods discovered during research into anaesthesia have also had an impact on how acute and chronic pain can be managed, even when no surgery is involved.

The museum has regular temporary exhibitions, exploring things like anaesthesia during war and the misuse of anaesthetic drugs, while the permanent displays explain the story of anaesthesia from the first public demonstration in 1846 right up to the present day. They have an exhaustive archive and library available to researchers, and the museum features thoughtfully constructed modern displays, with lots of photographs of those responsible for the development of the subject as well as a plethora of shiny steel surgical instruments in polished cases. They have also embraced the thrill of the 'drawer you can open', always a good thing in any museum. You can find out about the men in the photographs, their predecessors, and the search for effective pain relief, as well as experiments in resuscitation.

The museum's website includes a tour of nearby sites with connections to the subject – from Joseph Lister's house to the site of the first surgery under anaesthetic in Britain, if you're fired up by your new knowledge and fancy a walk.

....

anaesthesiaheritagecentre.org
The Association of Anaesthetists of Great Britain and Ireland
21 Portland Place, London W1B 1PY
e: heritage@aagbi.org   t: 020 7631 1650
Open: Mon–Fri 10am–4pm (last entry 3.30pm),
closed bank holidays
Free

Antique Breadboard Museum
London

In the heart of Putney, in a perfectly ordinary (if admittedly rather desirable) street, there's a house with a secret. You can't just barge in – this is a place where you need to make an appointment to visit.

It's not cheap to enter, but if you're even vaguely interested in British craftsmanship and social history (and scones, let's be honest – your ticket price includes afternoon tea) then it's worth every penny.

Although the idea of a museum of breadboards may seem perfect for any list of 'weird museums', it's really not that weird. It's one person's passion, but not the person you'll meet when you get there. This is Madeleine's house now, but it was once her mother's, and it was she who collected the boards over 40 years.

At first they appeared to be a rather awkward inheritance. Should they be sold? Given to the V&A? Or should she do what her mother (known to many as 'BB' for 'breadboard' – cute) had occasionally done and open her house to show off the collection? A photograph in an interiors magazine of a display of boards inspired her to get some up on the wall – the repetition of the circular boards, all the same yet all different, makes for a very pleasing focal point. And then it didn't seem such a stretch to imagine that people might want to come and look at them.

She started opening to the public in December 2017, making this the youngest museum in the book. You recognise the house by the breadboard hanging on the door. You come off the street into the front room of a Victorian terraced house, and there are the breadboards displayed on the walls and in a very fine glazed cabinet. More than just breadboards, in fact – there's a fantastic collection of breadknives with intricately carved handles as well, some stored in drawers that once held embroidery silk, plus butter dishes and even egg platters, a thing you may never have seen or heard of before.

BB was an antiques dealer, and she clearly had great taste; everywhere you look there are interesting and beautiful things. So there you are, staring around you at all the breadboards, many carved with ears of corn, fruit and flowers. And Madeleine will tell you all about them, opening the cabinet to show you the oldest objects in the collection, including a 17th-century trencher, scarred with the evidence of years of bread slicing, and the most fabulous wooden 'coaster'. Possibly used for cheese rather than bread, this has little wheels and would have been used to send food up and down the table. You are allowed to touch pretty much everything, being handed board after board so you can examine the detail and feel the wonderful patina of wooden objects that have lived long, useful lives.

The majority of the boards date from the mid-19th century, and you can trace their development as various design choices were made. At first they tended to be 'dished' – their design was based on ceramics, with 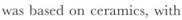 a slight dip in the middle – but this wasn't practical, as it meant you caught the knife on the carving round the edge when you sliced your bread. The centre needs to be raised slightly to avoid this. And what sort of wood is best for something that's going to get hard use? Sycamore is good. It's hardwearing and doesn't impart any flavour to the food you put on it. The biggest board manufacturers, Bramhall, were getting through 700 sycamore trees a year at their height. They continued to make breadboards until 2002.

BB did a lot of research on breadboards, which Madeleine has read, reviewed and filed, and plans to use as the basis for a book. She has copies of Victorian trade catalogues and examples of the actual boards illustrated. It's unexpectedly satisfying to turn the pages of drawings of boards and then hold one, comparing the illustration to the actual completed version, imagining perhaps that your great-great-grandmother might have perused similar pages.

Bread itself, of course, is an important thing, the staff of life, eternally the cheap and filling basis of the lives of countless farm and factory workers. Or was it? One of the reasons why breadboards suddenly became hugely fashionable in the mid-19th century was because bread, in fact, was not at all cheap after the end of the Napoleonic Wars. Protectionist legislation gave us the Corn Laws, and it wasn't until they were repealed in 1846 that bread was cheap and plentiful once again. And the Victorians were always looking for new and fashionable things to sell one another. Thus the demand for cheaply produced breadboards grew, and also for more expensive, luxury versions.

There's a box of antique breadboards to rummage through if you fancy starting your own collection, and if you have family recipes you want to share, or any titbits of teatime information, Madeleine will make a note for her blog. It's the engagement of the visitor with the collection that has proved valuable for her – everyone has bread-based memories, and breadboards are not intimidating or socially exclusive. Bring your gran's breadboard (or a photograph of it) to show her – she'll probably be able to tell you its approximate age. Breadboards were often given as wedding presents, and she even has one that was given, according to the carving, to somebody called Gertie by her cousin Walter as a 21st birthday present. As each letter of a bespoke carving would have cost money, this would have been quite a pricey gift, although history does not record what Gertie's reaction was. There are souvenir breadboards, a Mouseman breadboard, and a collection of fine modern hand-carved examples, their decoration rather more abstract than the standard ears of wheat or the letters 'BREAD' that adorn the majority.

If you've never really thought about breadboards – and they are the perfect example of something so ubiquitous that it's easy to never have considered them further than thinking you probably need one – you will learn so much that by the time the scones arrive you'll be happy to sit down for a rest. You get to choose a breadboard to have the scones served on – Madeleine is very keen for her visitors to interact with the exhibits – lay the table and drink tea while further discussing the Corn Laws, domestic life, and which supermarket makes the best scones. It is an extremely rewarding experience on every level.

....

antiquebreadboards.com
Lifford Street, Putney, London SW15 1NY
e: theantiquebreadboardmuseum@gmail.com   t: 020 8785 2464
Open: Tour and tea by appointment, book by phone or through Airbnb (airbnb.co.uk/experiences/126487)

Baked Bean Museum of Excellence

Port Talbot

Warning: This museum may contain fart jokes.

Is a museum dedicated to baked beans weird? Perhaps this depends on how you feel about baked beans; or perhaps it's intrinsically odd. Possibly it's the weirdest place in this book. And almost certainly the silliest – but there's nothing wrong with that.

Described as 'an outpost of cheerful craziness' by one satisfied customer, it's certainly quite an eccentric place. It's housed in the flat of the owner, Captain Beany. You'll need to phone in advance to make sure he's there and can accommodate your visit. Some people might find the personal attention of being escorted round rather too much, but if you're willing to embrace the experience you will be impressed by the levels of obsession found within. If nothing else, research for this book has demonstrated that nothing is ordinary if you look at it closely enough, and it's quite likely someone will. Even if you, the visitor, can't quite align your own interests with those of the curators, you have to respect their desire to find out all there is to know about their subject and share that knowledge with a wider world – and even, in this case, to wallpaper their flat in baked-bean orange, with Heinz blue as an accent, add orange carpets and wear suits of a similar colour, topped off with fabulous orange snakeskin boots, or, on less formal occasions, a shorts-and-T-shirt ensemble bedecked with enormous glistening beans.

Captain Beany wasn't always interested in beans, and he wasn't always called Captain Beany. For a long time he was plain Barry Kirk and he worked in IT at the BP chemical plant in Neath Port Talbot. Then, some 30-odd years ago, he set a new world record by sitting naked in a bath of baked beans for 100 hours. It was, as you might imagine, a life-changing experience. Thus he became Captain Beany, name changed by deed poll in 1991, and there was no looking back. A costume followed, as well as orange face paint. If you're going to do something like this, there is absolutely no point in being half-hearted about it. A golden cape is the least you can offer.

Captain Beany raises money for charity – lots of money – sometimes with traditional events like marathons, and sometimes with more esoteric options, such as having baked beans tattooed on his head, or using his nose to push a can of beans along a beach. The museum features a display of newspaper clippings and awards presented to the Captain for his fundraising. You might have seen him on the telly – he's a natural for anything about eccentrics.

Since 2009, his two-bedroom flat has been the only museum in the world dedicated to the humble baked bean. (Apparently Heinz once had a showroom with displays at their Pittsburgh factory, but no longer.) As you might expect, there are baked-bean tins from around the world, advertising ephemera and promotional material. Money boxes, posters, mugs, tea towels, jigsaw puzzles, egg cups, clocks… the entire flat is bean-themed. You might wonder what living in it would do to your brain, but Captain Beany is quite delightful, so maybe we could all do with more beans in our decor.

Baked beans have been manufactured in Britain since the early 20th century, but the original notion is American, of course – they were first produced commercially by Henry J Heinz in 1895. (By 1901 you could buy imported cans in Fortnum & Mason as a fancy and exotic treat.) Ironically, they're generally not baked at all, but stewed. Generally these days they're cooked in the can – raw beans and sauce are added, the can is sealed, and they're put in a huge pressure cooker. In the UK we like them cooked in tomato sauce, but Boston baked

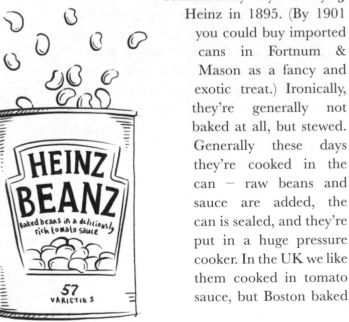

beans are made in a sauce of molasses and salt pork, and Quebec-style beans use maple syrup.

Where would the full English breakfast be without them? (See also the comfort of beans on toast – or beans to one side of the toast, depending on whether you like your toast soggy. This is clearly contentious, and views are very strongly held. Ask Captain Beany for his opinion.) The haricot bean is most commonly used to make baked beans – did you know that these are native to South America and first arrived in Europe in 1528? Considering this, it seems harsh that we had to wait 400 years for the apotheosis of bean convenience. In the UK, we eat more than a million cans a week, which is quite something.

Exhibits include a wide variety of brands you may never have heard of but which have long 'bean' (sorry!) popular in the States, like Bush's, and the glazed ceramic 'bean pots' in which the dish was traditionally cooked, as well as lots of collectable die-cast baked-bean delivery vehicles and a quite astonishing number of promotional Heinz objects. (Remember those rather disturbing 'beans pouring from a tin' statuettes?) Branston beans (because other people make beans as well, including HP and Batchelors, as well as all the supermarket own-brand versions) are mostly banished to the bathroom. When your visit is over you'll have a yearning to eat beans either immediately, or never again.

....

captainbeany.com/baked-bean-museum-of-excellence
6 Flint House, Moorland Road, Port Talbot, Wales SA12 6JX
e: bakedbeanmuseumofexcellence@captainbeany.com
t: 07803 872428
Open: Mon–Fri 10am–5pm (but phone in advance)
Free (donations welcome)

Bletchley Park

Milton Keynes

For decades following the end of World War II, no one talked about Bletchley Park. It was all still swathed in secrecy, the people who had worked there bound by the Official Secrets Act and unable to talk about their experiences.

Over the last 20 or so years all that has changed, and it's an internationally renowned visitor attraction and an established part of the story we tell ourselves about the war. A bunch of mostly posh, chess-playing, crossword-puzzle-solving maths types ('Dons and Debs') hidden away in a selection of huts and blocks in the grounds of an imposing Victorian mansion, cracking codes and aiding the war effort with the power of their brains. Of course, it's a bit more complex than that.

The site opened as a museum in 1993, having been saved from redevelopment. In 2014 it reopened after a multimillion-pound restoration. As with a lot of World War II sites, the buildings were never intended to last 70 years, and many of the huts in which so much of the work took place were in quite a precarious state. Now all are watertight once more and not so likely to be blown away by a stiff breeze.

Bletchley is often heralded as the 'birthplace of modern information technology', and it certainly played a vital role in the war – most famously, of course, as the place where the Enigma machine had its code cracked, allowing the Allies to read the messages the German armed forces and military command were sending. Interestingly, many of the weaknesses of the system were, as they say, user-generated if the enemy had been paying more attention, it would have been even harder to crack the ciphers, but there were a number of procedural flaws that really helped the process of decryption. The website is big on a celebration of the values of the codebreakers: 'broad-minded patriotism; commitment; discipline; technological excellence' – all of which are good things and we could probably do with more of them.

The stately home at the heart of the estate is an extravagant Victorian building with a copper cupola and a variety of roofscapes. Inside the house, the finely panelled rooms have been co-opted for the war effort. They are jammed with period details, from typewriters to telephones and desk lamps, uncomfortable-looking office chairs, filing cabinets, ashtrays and mugs, jackets hung on the backs of chairs, bags and briefcases under desks, all giving the impression that perhaps the people who sat at these desks have just popped out for some fresh air. There's a collection of vehicles – an ambulance, a Sunbeam Talbot sports saloon used in the 2001 film *Enigma*, a row of period bicycles, and motorcycles ridden by dispatch riders.

The huts are full of more mysterious objects – machinery of unknown purpose (or unknown until you read the interpretation boards, anyway). Although Enigma may be the most famous machine, there are plenty of others; the reconstruction of the Turing-Welchman Bombe, with its rows of dials, is perhaps the most physically impressive. (There are talks explaining how it works.) The Enigma machines themselves are rather smaller, though they, too, have a satisfying selection of keys and switches. They clearly do something clever, although you'd never be able to work out what. In the National Museum of Computing (which is on-site but separate, with its own entrance fee and opening hours; check the website at tnmoc.org for details), you can see Colossus – the world's first 'large electronic valve computer'. It's an immense beast, also used for codebreaking, which has been restored and left open so you can see the intricate mass of wires and relays inside it.

Alan Turing is probably Bletchley's most famous alumnus, and so the story of codebreaking is intertwined with his own story of injustice and tragedy. Hut 8 houses his office, complete with his mug, chained to the radiator, and is the place where he worked on the naval Enigma codes that were considered pretty well unbreakable, as well as others like the Lorenz cipher. (What's the difference between a code and a cypher? A code needs a code book. You can decide that 'Two pints of milk' means 'Enemy ships sighted' and then you can send an apparently innocuous message, and, as long as the person you're sending it to has the code book, they can interpret it correctly, but no one else can. A cypher, on the other hand, changes each letter or group of letters in a message to a combination of different letters, numbers and spaces. To interpret this, you need to know what each letter or number represents and how it's been transformed.)

The methods used for cracking the Enigma code are explained – although it's still quite complicated even with very clear diagrams and explanations. There are, it tells us, approximately 158 million million million (that's 18 zeros) 'possible electrical combinations' on a three-rotor Enigma machine. Interactive displays allow you to learn more about the various machines and how they worked.

Huts 3 and 6 were codebreaking huts, and it was here that the Enigma messages of the German army and air force were worked on. The huts are dressed to resemble the way they would have looked at the time, and there are various interpretive exhibits to give you an idea of what working here might have been like. The projected images and sounds are really well done, and you can listen to the real codebreakers tell their story.

Hut 11 housed the Turing-Welchman Bombe machines, and more film and interaction will help you get a grip on what went on here. The women who worked on the Bombe machines called this hut the 'Hell Hole', which suggests that it wasn't much fun.

The new displays have been thoughtfully put together and the whole place really is pretty fascinating. There's loads to look at – it's certainly a whole day out. There are lots of quotes from people who worked there, giving a real flavour of life on-site and how they saw their work. There are domestic displays as well, showing their living conditions.

Block C houses the visitor centre, which has an excellent exhibition exploring the site's history and importance.

And there's plenty of interactive stuff to keep the kids entertained. (There's a cafe in Hut 4, by the way.)

Also on-site is the National Radio Centre, where you can learn about the history of radio communications. It's run by the Radio Society of Great Britain, and admission is included in the Bletchley Park ticket price.

....

bletchleypark.org.uk

The Mansion, Bletchley Park, Sherwood Drive, Bletchley, Milton Keynes MK3 6EB

For sat nav use Sherwood Drive, Bletchley MK3 6DS

e: enquiries@bletchleypark.org.uk   t: 01908 640404

Open: Mar–Oct daily 9.30am–5pm (last entry 4pm);
Nov–Feb daily 9.30am–4pm (last entry 3pm)

Adults – £18.50 / children 12 to 17 – £10.75 /
children under 12 – free

British Dental Museum
London

If you've ever had a romantic notion that you'd have liked to live at some earlier point in history, you can soon shake yourself out of it with a visit to the British Dental Museum.

It's a tiny place, tucked into a corner at the headquarters of the British Dental Association in Wimpole Street, next to the Association's library, and open just two afternoons a week. The posters from the mid-20th century are jolly in tone: 'Have Clean Teeth and Smile All Day!', but most of the exhibits are decidedly grim, in a uniquely fascinating way. It is quite amazing to think about how your ancestors may have dealt with their dental emergencies. But if you're not wincing at the sight of clockwork drills and partial bridges made of real human teeth, then you're made of stern stuff. Even the toothbrushes – whether ivory, bone or silver – are disconcerting.

The collection was begun in 1919, when Lillian Lindsay, the first woman to qualify as a dentist in the UK, donated some old dental instruments to the BDA. She'd been keeping them in a box under her bed, as you do. The collection now numbers some 30,000 items, not all of which are on display. Originally intended mostly for members of the Association, the museum has been open to the public since 1967, undergoing a redesign in the mid-2000s. It's a modern, well-designed use of the compact space. There's plenty to read, and an audio tour as well if you want to know more about the history of this most essential branch of medicine. No one (or hardly anyone) enjoys a trip to the dentist, but we all know it's a mistake to avoid check-ups. At least if you have toothache today you don't have to be held down in a chair while someone who more usually cuts hair grapples with a pair of pliers in the tender recesses of your mouth.

One of the most interesting things about the development of the science of dentistry is the connected development of pain relief. A visit to the Anaesthesia Museum (see page 15), just round the corner in Portland Place, will tell you even more, but the Dental Museum explains how vital the discovery of ether, chloroform and – most importantly – nitrous oxide proved to be, allowing pain-free (although not risk-free, as the gases are dangerous in themselves) treatment and extractions. Nitrous oxide's reputation as a 'party drug' (people took it for fun on its first discovery) hampered its acceptance as a method of anaesthetic, unfortunately – to the undoubted discomfort of many.

If you have dentists in your family tree, the museum can help with research (for a donation) using the Dentists Registers, which began in 1879. The registers started in response to the Dentists Act of 1878, the first legislation that restricted who could offer dental advice and treatment. In order to register, you had to be qualified – surely a relief to every patient. Exams followed training, which would usually include making dentures as well as study and clinical practice. Only if you were listed in the register could you call yourself a 'dental surgeon'. Unfortunately, some people recognised a handy loophole – what if you called yourself something else, or merely offered 'dental treatment'? You could carry on as before without qualifying. This loophole was closed in 1921, after which you could not practise if you weren't qualified – although you could register, unqualified, if you could prove you'd been working as a dentist prior to 1921. (The last dentist without qualifications in this sense was still working in the 1970s.)

The collection includes dental chairs which might be polished wood and velvet but don't look as reassuringly medical as the sort of thing your dentist has now – although the 1960s/1970s version in the lobby might be more nostalgic. And, of course, there are all the expected drills and picks and other things that will make you flinch. There are anatomical models, used for teaching and to allow students to get some practice with their tools before plunging into a live mouth. There's also a nice collection of prints and paintings with a dental theme, including a number of Georgian cartoons by Cruikshank and Rowlandson. These are of interest because they show social attitudes to dental work and teeth in general, illustrating who might be expected to carry out such work before dentists really existed – the local blacksmith, perhaps – and also what was fashionable. The development of new types of dentures often caused much hilarity, which seems a bit harsh, but there you go.

There's a cabinet full of dentures and partial dentures to wince at, including some 'Waterloo teeth' (so-called because they were sometimes made from the teeth of soldiers killed in battle). These were quite the thing in the early 19th century, as human teeth look more, well, human than those carved from the ivory of unfortunate elephants, hippos or walruses – and they last better too. A market for human teeth tends to result in dubious behaviour, so some proud owners of a fine new set might unknowingly be showing off teeth from recently disinterred corpses. It's probably best not to dwell on this thought in a world without effective methods of sterilisation. Sometimes rich people paid for the teeth of poor people to be removed and inserted into their own gums – something that makes even the worst kind of dentures seem like a much better bet. You'll not be surprised to hear that someone else's teeth very rarely make a comfortable new home in your mouth. Also, if the former owner of the teeth was suffering from syphilis, guess what? This is a much less entertaining way of becoming infected than the standard method.

For most people there was no real notion of preventative dental care until the 20th century. People did brush their teeth, of course, and the museum has examples of various toothbrushes and oral hygiene sets, the fancier of which resemble manicure sets, with mother-of-pearl handles and silver-gilt detailing. One of the problems was that the tooth powders available were extremely abrasive, so even those people who were paying attention were likely to be damaging their teeth while they tried to look after them. By the 1920s, oral health was considered a more general social issue, and advertising campaigns were more common. Some of this was commercial, with companies promoting their own products. The national Dental Board, meanwhile, appealed to the patriotic citizen, afraid that bad oral health could lead to 'civil unrest, lightning strikes and Bolshevism' – and no one wants that.

All in all, this little museum is likely to make you pathetically grateful to your own dentist, and extremely relieved that your own teeth get the benefits of 21st-century dentistry.

....

bda.org/museum
64 Wimpole Street, London W1G 8YS
e: museum@bda.org   t: 020 7563 4549
Open: Tue & Thu 1–4pm
Free

British Lawnmower Museum
Merseyside

Along with the Derwent Pencil Museum (see page 72), this is probably one of the best known of the 'unusual museums', a perennial member of any list of the unexpected collection.

As well as exploring the history of this most ubiquitous piece of garden machinery, it also features lawnmowers of famous people, which is fun, although you do have to wonder whether Prince Charles, for example, ever actually used the one he owned. Jean Alexander (who played Hilda Ogden in *Coronation Street*) was the first celebrity to donate a machine – her 1950s Qualcast. It's always interesting to see non-glamorous things that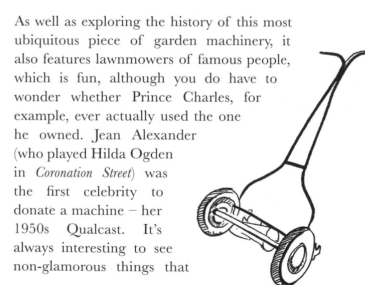

have belonged to the rich and famous. As you gawp at machines once belonging to Brian May or Eric Morecambe, you can try to imagine what their gardens might be like, and whether they were enthusiastic mowers of lawns or the kind who had to be encouraged. Did they return from their holidays (or tours, or whatever) to find the grass up to their knees?

In the past, lawns weren't really a thing, and when they became popular in the 18th century they were the preserve of the wealthy, who had their grassy swards trimmed by men with scythes. Later, ponies with leather shoes (no one wants hoofprints offending the eye, after all) pulled mowing machines, and the first patent for a lawnmower was taken out in 1830 by Edwin Beard Budding (a nice bit of gardening-related nominative determinism there). He worked in a textile mill in Stroud, and the idea for the lawnmower developed from a machine that trimmed the nap from cloth. He thought it could be used for cutting grass; everyone else thought he was mad. His machine was designed to mow large areas of grass in parks and sports grounds – London Zoo bought one of the earliest ones. It was a two-man machine – one pushing and the other pulling. Another 60 years would pass before anyone built a steam-powered one, but Budding's system – the cylinder-cutting principle – is still the one used by many machines today. Without his vision, perhaps, the lawn would never have been something within the reach of ordinary people, and summer Sundays in suburbia would sound very different. (Mr Budding also invented the adjustable spanner. Not everyone has a lawn, but an adjustable spanner is always useful, so all hail EBB.)

The museum is the life's work and passion of Brian Radam (aka the Lawn Ranger), scion of a family lawnmower business, former lawnmower-racing champion and expert on all things lawnmower-related. The Radam family became involved with lawnmowers in 1945, when the business that became Lawnmowerworld began. Brian himself worked as an apprentice at well-known British mower company Atco, where he repaired more than 400 mowers a week. He's written books about them, including the Haynes' *Lawnmower Manual*, and it's because of his love for the machine that the museum exists.

The museum is part of Lawnmowerworld, which sells lawnmowers and parts for lawnmowers, and will service or fix your mower should you require it. If you inherit an elderly model, or find one in the shed at your new house and fancy learning more about it, this is the place to come; these people are experts, valuing antique machines and curating a huge archive of advertising and instructional ephemera.

They have around 1,000 mowers, 200 of which are on display and have been fully restored. These include tiny (but functional) versions, a solar-powered robot mower, examples of the first Atco, Flymo and Ransom machines, and Victorian and other historic mowers. A recent acquisition is the original mower from Lord's Cricket Ground, one of the most expensive lawnmowers in the world at the time of its purchase. (You could have bought a house for the same money.)

Brian (and, by extension, the museum) is a leading authority on vintage mowers of all kinds, as well as other vintage and antique garden machinery. His aim is to preserve these machines for posterity, a reminder of the time when British lawnmowers were the best in the world.

To get the most from your visit, a guided tour is probably essential. As well as learning all about the wide variety of exhibits at the museum, you can probably pick up some tips for looking after your own lawn, if you have one.

....

lawnmowerworld.co.uk

106–112 Shakespeare Street, Southport, Merseyside PR8 5AJ

e: info@lawnmowerworld.com   t: 01704 501336

Open: Mon–Sat 9am–5.30pm

Adults – £3 / children – £1

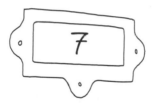

British Optical Association Museum

London

The College of Optometrists is found in a fine Georgian building near Charing Cross. Back in the 1820s it housed a dealership importing 'telescopes, kaleidoscopes and other optical toys' – which seems appropriate.

The College isn't full of students; it's the home of the professional body that oversees the nation's ophthalmic opticians (also known as optometrists). It's also home to the museum of the British Optical Association, founded in 1901 and recognised as the world's oldest optical museum. The Association, like many of the new professional medical bodies formed in the late 19th century, was keen to have London premises and a library, and it wasn't long before members were donating antique spectacles and other items. By 1926 the museum was open to the public, and it remained so, on and off (various moves and a war rather interfering), until the move to the current premises in 1997 allowed for a more permanent and professional display.

Just a few doors down the street is the former home of Benjamin Franklin – supposedly the inventor of, among other things, the split bifocal lens. Whether this is true or not is up for debate, but you might also learn some rather eye-opening (sorry!) facts about him during your visit.

Depending on how you feel about eyes, this is less disturbing than the British Dental Museum (see page 36) – nothing's grimmer than toothache, after all – but just as fascinating. There's loads to read, plenty to learn, and the curator, Neil Handley, will show you round. If you have time, it's strongly recommended that you take the extended tour. Two hours might seem like a long time to spend being told about glasses but there's so much to see, and Neil knows pretty much all there is to know about the objects in his care.

The aim of the collection is to curate anything connected with eyes in any way, so as well as optical instruments, spectacle frames and the wonderful collection of paintings and prints, there's a collection of generally 'eye-themed' objects, from the cyclopic mascots of the 2012 Olympics to beautiful 'eye portraits' – discreet and subtle mementos exchanged between lovers, popular in the 18th century.

In fact, the collection is home to more than 27,000 items (not all on display), including the late Queen Mother's specs, a pair belonging to Ronnie Corbett, and even some dating from 1784 that belonged to Samuel Johnson. There's a wonderful case of glass eyes, too, dating to World War I. Glass eyes are really beautiful – if a little creepy, perhaps – and the skill involved in creating the colours of the iris and even the tiny thread veins in the white is remarkable. The museum is crammed with objects. The walls are festooned with advertising posters and the cases are full of often very attractive as well as interesting items, like the collection of eyebaths, which come in many shades of blue and green glass, as well as some more unusual porcelain versions. Look out for the one with the Phrygian cap, from Revolutionary France.

If you wear glasses or contact lenses (and even if you don't yet, one day you probably will), you've probably wondered what your life would be like if you'd lived at a time before corrective eyewear. It's reasonably comforting to know that people have been attempting to improve things for those of us with visual impairments for hundreds of years – spectacles were first developed in the 13th century, and the earliest examples 'for continuous wear' (rather than, say, reading glasses for specific uses) on display date from the early 1700s.

If you enjoy the thrill of all the different machines when you go to the optician, you'll see some early versions here, as well as some of those lovely boxes of lenses that always seem so appealing.

The museum explores the development of optometry and eyewear, as well as optical instruments such as telescopes (they have some fantastic 18th- and 19th-century examples of these). Check out the sunglasses from the 1780s, worn by a Venetian gondolier to avoid glare from the lagoon. Or if that's not thrilling enough, they also have some sunglasses that belonged to Rihanna. The strangest exhibit is probably the eyewear for chickens, meant to stop them pecking each other.

An extended tour begins upstairs, where the paintings displayed in various meeting rooms (this is a working building, so there may be rooms you can't access) demonstrate how the spectacle-wearer was initially seen as a potentially dubious character. A selection of misers, money-changers and shockingly godless old people illustrate this. Improving your eyesight was clearly the behaviour of the morally dubious – at least to begin with. It's interesting to see this attitude changing, as the brave (Vice Admiral Peter Rainier, who served in the Napoleonic Wars), the fashionable (Sir Joshua Reynolds) and the saintly (St Jerome) were portrayed (or portrayed themselves, in Reynolds' case) in their specs. St Jerome's are fictional – glasses hadn't been invented when he was translating the Bible into Latin in the 4th century. Suggesting that he owned a pair, though, shows that they now signified wisdom and knowledge, rather than indicating wickedness.

The tour then descends (via the library – check out the eye tests in Japanese, Hebrew and Arabic) to the basement, where two rooms are crammed with exhibits. There's so much to look at it's lucky you have someone with you to point out the best bits. Neil will explain why they have a stuffed turtle, and more about the history of the collection. You'll also get some time on your own to go back round and make sure you didn't miss anything. Highlights include the National Health frames that will be painfully familiar to anyone over 45, and a remarkable collection of contact lenses through the ages. Devices like the frightening glasses with multiple lenses that allow partially sighted people to drive in the US are remarkable – and they even have a pair of Daniel Radcliffe's Harry Potter frames from the first film, *Harry Potter and the Philosopher's Stone*. (These are tungsten, as apparently DR is allergic to nickel, which the original frames were made from.)

Don't miss the narrow chest of drawers filled with antique and vintage frames that you can try on – oh joy! Make sure you leave yourself enough time to fully embrace this opportunity.

Oh – and the building is supposed to be haunted, so keep, as they say, an eye out.

....

college-optometrists.org/the-college/museum.html

The College of Optometrists, 42 Craven Street, London WC2N 5NG

e: museum@college-optometrists.org   t: 020 7766 4353

Open: Mon–Fri 9am–5pm (by appointment and guided tour only)

Standard Tour – free, lasts about 40 minutes; Full Building Tour – £5, lasts two hours

Use the booking system on the website to request an appointment, and they'll get back to confirm/discuss arrangements – do not turn up at the museum without a firm confirmation of booking!

British Vintage Wireless and Television Museum
London

Even if you've prepared yourself for a visit to this discreetly located museum by looking at pictures on the internet, you won't quite have been able to imagine how it actually feels to stand in a large shed surrounded by vintage radios. It's overwhelming, in a wonderful way.

Radios used to be furniture, beautifully styled, in carved and polished wood. A sturdy radiogram could take up a whole shelf and weigh as much as a small child. The dial, printed with the names of stations across Europe, gave a glimpse of a world outside your own front room.

You'll need to have phoned to make an appointment – this is another museum where there's no opportunity to just pop in as you're passing. As with the other appointment-only establishments in this book, you should absolutely not allow that to put you off. Phone them now and arrange a visit.

Once again you're in the presence of an obsession. In this case, the obsession of the late Gerry Wells. What you see around you is Gerry's life's work. As a kid during the Blitz, he'd seek out abandoned radios and other electrical equipment in bomb-damaged houses, just as Thomas Rushton would look for sewing machines (see page 125). The same urge to rescue machinery surely drove them both. Later in life – in the early 1970s, as people began to throw out their old machines and replace them with something smaller and more modern, maybe with transistors instead of valves – he began rescuing radios again. Gerry couldn't pass a radio in a skip without taking it home with him, and soon his house was full of them. In 1974 he began opening his fledgling museum to the public.

He repaired radios for other people, too, which led to one of the most unexpected turns of an unusual life. John Paul Getty – yes, that John Paul Getty – owned one of the earliest radiograms. It needed fixing, and Gerry was recommended as the expert's expert. He fixed the radiogram and charged his usual rate of around £70, which, unsurprisingly, Getty found rather intriguing. If you're one of the world's richest men, people generally bung a couple of quid on their prices. Not Gerry, though. This led to Getty sending his secretary out to Dulwich for a look, and the report he got back fired his curiosity further. Getty bought extra land for an extension to the museum, paid its utility bills, and even visited himself.

When Gerry died in 2014 it wasn't certain that the museum could continue. The house was sold and converted into flats, which meant that all the radios that had been kept there needed to be moved out to the sheds. There wasn't enough room for all of them, and many had to be sold. Some of them were even thrown away, their rescue only temporary. Don't panic, though – there are still hundreds. More than you could ever really look at in one visit. Luckily, the staff are keen and enthusiastic guides, and will take you round and point out the ones you should be paying particular attention to. This isn't really a museum with labels – most of the information is held in the heads of the curators, who are entertaining and full of facts.

You may have vaguely wondered why the 'wireless' is thus named, when they obviously have loads of wires, but it's nothing to do with the wires in your set, or the ones that connect it to the electrical supply; it's about the link between the broadcaster and the receiver. If you're communicating by telegraph, you have to be physically linked by a wire in order to broadcast your message.

The exhibits illustrate the entire history of the radio, even if the curators aren't quite so fussed about the new ones. Following the story of 'the wireless' from crystal sets to DAB is fascinating, though, watching the sets change in style and size, seeing how every generation has its own notion of modernity, which is soon old hat, before eventually becoming retro-vintage and cool once again.

There's a room full of televisions, too, and how strange it is to see them with their greyish glass-fronted screens and fat, cathode-ray tube-concealing bodies. If you take a young person with you, they'll be amazed at how small they are and how very unflat the screens. Many of these still work, and it's strangely exciting when they turn them on, even if they are showing modern telly instead of, say, *Corrie* in black and white or a nice episode of *Crown Court*. This is the only place in the country where you can watch working vintage TVs – they have a special converter to allow this, and if you're technically minded the television curators will explain how this works. They're just as friendly and knowledgeable as the chaps who look after the radios. By the way, if you've ever noticed a television or radio in a period film or drama, it was probably loaned by the museum – that's how they make most of their money.

In addition to tellies and radios, there's a wide collection of catalogues, advertising and paper ephemera everywhere, vintage lightbulbs (for inside the radios to light up the dial), mains connectors and some very fine mid-century glass lightshades, hanging above the radios. There's an excellent display of valves, which is a lot more pleasing than it maybe sounds. There are old batteries, lamps, the old two-pin plugs used before the standardised versions that we use now, microphones, and a collection of gifts given by radio and TV reps to the dealers they hoped would sell their products to a public greedy for sound and vision. This is a wonderful place and you could spend hours and hours in the softly lit sheds with their aroma of dust and electricity.

....

bvwtm.org.uk/index.htm

23 Rosendale Road, West Dulwich, London SE21 8DS

Access to the museum is via the green side gate,
not the front door of the house

t: 020 8670 3667

Open: By appointment only

Suggested donation of £10 per adult

Bubble Car Museum
Lincolnshire

Bubble cars! An iconic (if unsung) part of motoring and social history and also super-cute. At the Bubble Car Museum they have a collection of more than 50, as well as various scooters and motorcycles (some microcars, like the Reliant, could be driven on a motorcycle licence).

There's nothing better than a museum that really goes all out with a collection that specialises in one or two things – and it's always good when those things are enormously photogenic.

You've probably seen examples of the bubble car on TV – Jeremy Clarkson famously drove a Peel P50 (the smallest car ever to go into production)

into a lift at Television Centre during the third-most-watched episode of *Top Gear* – but you might not have ever seen one in 'real life', in which case get yourself to Lincolnshire pronto.

Although there had always been a market for small, low-cost vehicles, the technology for these little beauties was really developed during the period of post-war austerity and they became even more popular and useful when the Suez Crisis of 1956 instigated increases in petrol prices.

These machines, also known as 'microcars', are 700cc or smaller – some much smaller – and were very fuel efficient. They were often produced by small, local manufacturers as well as larger companies – German ex-aircraft producers, such as Messerschmitt and Heinkel, developed some of the first examples, and gave them their nickname, derived from the cockpit-like design of the canopies. Their lightweight nature allowed for an unusual, futuristic look when compared with the traditional vehicles of the time. The Italians got in on the action, too, licensing the Isetta to be built in the UK (where it had one rear wheel instead of two, to make the best of the three-wheeled vehicle laws). The French made tiny *'voiturettes'*, too, but these weren't exported. British manufacturers saw an opportunity and soon they were making tiny, odd little cars all over the country as well.

Bond, based in Lancashire, were one of the best-known English makers, along with Berkeley of Biggleswade, whose design ethic was taken from the sports cars of the time. Others included the Meadows Frisky, the Trident and P50 from the Peel Engineering Company on the Isle of Man, Reliant, AC Petite and Scootacar.

During the 1960s they were marketed as cheap and fun, quirky alternatives to duller, more conventional vehicles. Later versions moved on from the 'bubble' look to a more wedge-like appearance, but by the end of the decade their popularity was on the wane, with competition from a new generation of small cars, including the Mini. You can get four adults in a Mini, after all, and it won't tip over if you take a corner too fast. There was still a market until the 1980s, though, and the museum includes a Bamby, a single-seater made in Hull in the early 1980s.

Probably the most instantly recognisable microcar is the Reliant Regal Supervan, famous wherever *Only Fools and Horses* is shown in perpetuity (so probably everywhere). If you want to buy one of these, you'll find it hard to avoid ones that have been repainted with 'Trotters Independent Trading Co.'

At the museum, as well as the vehicles – some arranged in dioramas (and who doesn't love a diorama – the camping one is particularly pleasing, with its tiny plywood caravan and retro picnic gear) – there are large collections of vintage objects. These include some Bakelite, loads of 'Heirloom' pattern Hornsea Pottery (made not so far away in East Yorkshire) and a number of dinky little room settings. Check out the mid-century modern look in the 1950s sitting room, and the display of kitchenalia in the kitchen. There's an archive upstairs with a great collection of advertising and technical books, manuals and papers, and a tea shop as well. There's also a 'barn finds' section of rusty old unloved vehicles to fill you with anticipation about how they might one day be restored.

These are very much the sort of cars that have fans, and the museum is often host to rallies held by various owners' clubs (there's a campsite as well), so you might get to see even more examples if you choose the right day to visit.

And don't forget, if you book in advance and the weather is favourable, you can take a ride in one of the roadworthy examples. Do it – you'll be kicking yourself if you don't make a booking and then see other people enjoying this treat.

....

bubblecarmuseum.co.uk

Clover Farm, Main Road, Langrick, Boston, Lincolnshire PE22 7AW

t: 01205 280037

Open: Mar–Nov (check website for details)

Adults – £4 / children – £1

Bubble car rides (additional fee) must be pre-booked and are weather-dependent

Clearwell Caves

Gloucestershire

These days, Clearwell Caves is a kind of multi-purpose visitor attraction, with show caves, bats and living history, but the reason we've listed it here is because of the history of the site.

As you may know, iron ore and coal can be found beneath the Forest of Dean, and the exploitation of these resources has been going on for centuries, generally on quite a pre-industrial scale. Only certain people – the free miners – can mine here, and this has been the case for more than a thousand years. This is a birthright, so you can't just 'join'; you have to be born here.

The late Ray Wright, who first began to open the caves to the public in the late 1960s, was secretary of the Royal Forest of Dean Freeminers' Association for more than 30 years, and his son, Jonathan, now takes that role. These caves have been producing iron ore and ochre (coloured minerals that are also a form of iron) since at least the Bronze Age. Ochre might not be such an important resource these days — but 4,500 years ago it was probably what sent miners into the caves in the first place. If you're used to a more commercial kind of show cave, this is rather low-key, but they do have lighting effects and projections and so on.

It's recommended that you wear something sensible on your feet when you visit — a flat sole with some grip is your best bet. And make sure you bring a jumper, as the temperature is a constant 10°C.

But first, a bit of geology. What makes the Forest of Dean special? It's a natural basin, formed by 300 million-year-old Carboniferous rocks, which overlie Devonian Old Red Sandstone (which isn't necessarily red, by the way). In the centre of the forest, these rocks include shales and coal-bearing sandstones. The iron ore is found beneath these, in Carboniferous limestone. This limestone is what you'll see as outcropping cliffs around the edge of the basin. It's the iron ore-bearing rocks that form the caves — limestone, of course, being your prime material for any kind of cave you might want to climb down into, eroded gradually by the rainwater seeping into it. Rainwater is weakly acidic and eventually, over millions of years, dissolves the rock. Other well-known show caves, like Wookey Hole, White Scar in North Yorkshire and Aillwee Cave in County Clare in the Republic of Ireland, are all limestone systems.

The landscape round here was markedly different in the past. Although it's almost impossible to get your head round the idea, it was a desert during the Late Triassic. The iron ore had already formed, but the caves got a kick start at this point as occasional immense storms, with prolonged and torrential rain, dissolved the iron on the surface. The resulting acidic water carved out the caves, leaving iron ore deposits. Further upheaval pushed the land surface up higher as the local rivers (or, rather, the ancestors of local rivers) cut through some of the ancient cave systems, exposing the ore. There are various former river tributaries, visible as dry valleys, all over the area.

At first, people would have picked up iron ore from these surface deposits, but soon they were following it deeper underground. For thousands of years the people who did this were, presumably, whoever happened to be around, and whoever was able to recognise iron ore or ochre when they saw it. By around the 10th century AD, however, these resources were valuable enough to require regulation, and so the rights of the free miners began. The rules, as ratified in the Dean Forest (Mines) Act of 1838, are that you have to have been born and be living within the Hundred of St Briavels, you have to be over 21, and you have to have worked for a year and a day in a coal or iron mine within the Hundred. Oh, and you have to be male, or you did until 2010, when they (finally) amended the rules to allow women to be free miners. You register for a 'gale' or working anywhere in the Hundred (except under churchyards, gardens or orchards), and then you can mine for iron ore, stone, coal and associated minerals.

As you travel through the caves, there are displays explaining the activities and lives of the miners from the earliest days right up to the present. The story of the children who worked in the mines until the early 20th century is particularly eye-opening.

The caves were among the earliest producers of ochre in the British Isles, and the pigment is thought to have been mined here for more than 7,000 years (since the Mesolithic era – they have stone tools dated to 4,500 years ago. Ochre pigment is found as a soft deposit mixed in with the harder crystalline iron ore, and was particularly significant for people in prehistory, frequently being associated with funerary assemblages (in Europe it's found in examples of cave art, although the British cave art discovered so far is scratched rather than painted). Yellow, orange, brown, red and purple ochre are still mined here, dug by hand using simple tools. The ochre is sieved, washed and milled, before being mixed with various substances to make paints. Until the 1930s, Forest of Dean mines were famous for their ochre, particularly shades of red and purple.

There's archaeological evidence for the extraction of ochre pigments before 2,500 BC, and, by the time the Romans arrived, iron and coal working was already extensive. It's been suggested that the relationship between the miners and their new bosses might be the origin of the free-mining system, allowing them to operate without direct imperial control. By the time of the Norman Conquest, iron ore from the forest was a significant contributor to the national economy, and the miners were a highly regarded and privileged group. They were frequently involved in military campaigns, because their expertise underground could be very useful during sieges. Working as 'sappers' during the Hundred Years' War and beyond, they undermined fortifications and built earthworks.

Once the Industrial Revolution was in full swing, things began to change for the miners. Suddenly everyone was interested in their coal and iron, and there was a lot of pressure to industrialise and allow 'outsiders' to get involved. To mine the deeper measures, outside investment was required, it was suggested, by powerful people who stood to make a a great deal of money out of it. There were a lot of dubious shenanigans, including the theft of the Mine Law Court records by Crown officials. Without records, the court could no longer operate, to the outrage of the miners.

The result of a royal commission in 1831 to inquire into the 'nature of the mineral interests and freemining customs of the Forest of Dean' was the passing of the Dean Forest (Mines) Act, which confirmed the free miners' exclusive right to the minerals.

When the coal mines were nationalised after World War II, the Forest of Dean was exempt, due to the unique nature of its history and customs. Although some of the larger collieries underwent compulsory purchase, they were still held under the free-mining system and a royalty was paid.

Today there are around 150 free miners and a handful of small collieries still operating, along with one iron mine, Clearwell Caves itself.

If the show caves and their mining history are not thrilling enough for you, there are further opportunities here involving crawling and hard hats. There are two options: one is semi-deep caving, exploring beyond the public tour route with a guide who can tell you what you're looking at and make sure you don't get lost. This is a good tour for children who are keen to do a bit more clambering, and lasts about two hours. If this, too, seems unadventurous, you can do some deep-level caving, descending 200 feet beneath the ground. This is a bit more hardcore, and lasts three hours. Once again you're out with a guide – there are more than 600 acres of passageways and caverns beneath the forest, and you wouldn't want to get lost. Your guide will discuss what sort of creeping, crawling and climbing your group would like to do. More educational tours are also available, with an emphasis on Victorian mining, perhaps, or local geology.

....

clearwellcaves.com

Nr Coleford, Gloucestershire GL16 8JR

t: 01594 832535

Open: Apr–Aug daily 10am–5pm; Feb–Mar & Sep–Oct daily 10am– 4pm (see website for exact dates)

In December the caves are dressed for Christmas (see website for details)

Adults – £7.50 / children 4 to 16 – £5.50 /children under 4 – free (see website for prices for longer tours)

Cuckooland
Cheshire

Maybe the pleasure found in cuckoo clocks is similar to that of dolls' houses. Anything intricate is enticing, and Black Forest woodcarving is nothing if not intricate. In addition, the secret life of the cuckoo itself, usually (although not always) tucked away until the clock chimes, goes a long way to explain why these clocks have always been so popular.

Although you may have seen a display of five or six, perhaps, in a shop – or more, if you've visited their German homeland – there's no denying that the mass of clocks at Cuckooland is pretty impressive, almost overwhelming. It's no surprise to find that this unique collection is perhaps the most important in the world. There are around 700 clocks here, with their pinecone weights, glossy dark wood, carved leaves and flowers, and a lot of ticking. And plenty of cuckooing, of course, from clocks that call the quarter hours as well as the hours.

The Piekarski brothers, Roman and Maz, own and run the place. They're experienced horologists and clock restorers (if you've got a cuckoo clock with problems, they can look at it for you) and they've been studying and collecting clocks since their teens, drawn to the complexity and beauty of the Black Forest's most famous export. The first clock the brothers bought was a rare parquetry-style clock made around 1850, and since then they've travelled all over the world while adding to their collection, which became large enough to be shared with the public in 1990. They reset the whole lot twice a year as British Summer Time begins and ends – imagine! (Photos of them doing so are very popular with the local and even the national press on occasions like the centenary of BST.)

Generally, the impression you get when you enter the museum is quite a brown and woody one, but some colour is added by the bright paint of the rare German 'keyless concert organ' (pipe organ), built to play loudly at fairs and markets, as well as the flags that hang from the ceiling, and by the brothers' collection of vintage motorbikes. There's a fascinating display of traditional tools as well, with a vast number of steel rules and pliers, and you won't just see cuckoos – the clocks are decorated with many other kinds of birds and animals, as well as stunning foliage and flowers. There are also other examples of Black Forest carvings, including a boar with a very cheeky grin. There are quail clocks (they have quails instead of cuckoos, you'll be surprised to hear), trumpeter clocks (which feature a little bugler or trumpeter), clocks with carved bell towers that open to show monks ringing monastery bells, and so on.

Many of the clocks on show are extremely rare. They have lots by Johann Baptist Beha (1815–98), who was one of the most famous Black Forest clockmakers, responsible for various innovations in the form. They also have modern examples by famous international designers, and a 'cuckoo and echo' clock that might be one of only six in the world. It uses bellows and whistles to recreate more accurately the sounds the bird makes in the wild.

There's some debate about when (and by whom) the cuckoo clock was first devised, but apparently Philipp Hainhofer (1578–1647), a diplomat/banker/art collector from Augsburg in Bavaria, was the first person to write a description of one. Whoever invented them, they clearly struck a chord with the inhabitants of the Black Forest, and by the mid-19th century there were a number of clockmakers producing them, most notably in the little town of Furtwangen. The extravagantly carved versions known as Bahnhäusle (railway house – these are the 'classic' version) and Jagdstück (hunting scene – these are the ones with deer's heads and hunting rifles) soon became extremely popular, not just locally but throughout Europe.

Rather ironically, Cuckooland doesn't keep regular hours, so you would do best to call or email to set up a visit or a tour. They'll be happy to hear from you – if they can make out what you're saying over the cuckoos, the ticking, and the organ.

cuckoolandmuseum.com
The Old School, Chester Road, Tabley, Cheshire WA16 OHL
e: cuckoolanduk@btinternet.com   t: 01565 633039 /
07946 511661 / 07507 672931
Open: Visits by arrangement only (telephone in advance)

Dennis Severs' House

London

Spitalfields is a fascinating place, even now, when much of it is cleaned up and gentrified and a lot of the crumpled dirty pleasure of it has been chased away, replaced by modern buildings and fancy places to eat.

There remain a good number of elegant 18th-century houses, though, built for the Huguenot silk weavers who lived and worked here. These are not the houses of rich people − or at least that's not who they were built for. The silk weavers were middle class. In the 1970s and 1980s the houses were dilapidated and unadmired, many of them at risk of demolition and destruction, but now they are restored and desirable. Here on Folgate Street stands No. 18 − black front door, red shutters, gas lamp glowing, and a queue of people. A Sunday afternoon or Monday lunchtime visit is cheaper than coming in the evening, but you can't book then − you must turn up hopefully and see whether you'll be lucky.

They let in just 10 visitors at a time, every 20 minutes or so. Inside, the rule is 'silence', so make sure you've done all your talking before they open the door and let you in. You'll hear a brief explanation of what awaits you within and you're encouraged to take the time to listen and pause, imagining as well as looking, while you journey through the rooms.

Inside it's dark, even in daylight and even in summer – the rooms lit only by candlelight and the filtered daylight that makes its way through the windows, half-shuttered, draped and obscured. First, descend the stairs to the basement kitchen down in the shadows, where on hot summer days, the remains of a fire might make the atmosphere very close. The candles are reflected in the glittering china on the dresser; a sugarloaf stands on the table. The thick glass in the windows distorts the legs of the people queuing above you, waiting to enter the house. A clock ticks, the floorboards creak. It is almost magical, even to a cynic.

Then you climb back up through the house, exploring the other rooms – seeing a meal abandoned in the dining room, a cup of tea on the table in the parlour, rumpled sheets, an overturned chair, washing hung to dry. And everywhere letters and pictures and mirrors and china and detail after endless detail. There's more to look at than you can ever hope to take in.

And what's the point? The point is to engage with the fantasy as conceived by the late Mr Severs, who spent many years collecting the objects you see around you and arranging them, like the background of a 'still-life drama', to create the atmosphere of mystery and slowly passing time that he hoped his visitors would enjoy. His intention was that you 'enter his house... as if you have passed through the surface of a painting'.

He created the imaginary weavers – the Jervis family – who inhabit the house, and used 'their' belongings to tell stories or to help you tell stories yourself, as you progress through the rooms. The creak of the stairs, the darkness, the warmth, the endless years, the dust and cobwebs, the hair in the ivory comb on the dressing table – all of these things are very evocative, but you may find the smells are what affect you most: beeswax, paper, tobacco and oranges. It's probably not for everyone – it's not a straightforward experience, nor is it a standard museum. It's a bit pretentious, too – 'You either see it, or you don't' is perhaps not a very inclusive motto. You have to let your mind wander in a particular way; and, despite seeing a thousand wonderful vignettes, you mustn't take photos. This forces you to experience everything in the moment, rather than later when you look at your pictures. You might find this surprisingly distressing – there are a million Instagrammable details. How else can you capture the feeling of late August sunshine falling heavy on the staircase? Better write some notes.

Mr Severs' own story is just as interesting as that of any imaginary weaver, too – he lived in the house with various assistants and companions, and entertained exuberantly. This surely means that there must be a bathroom hidden somewhere. His friends felt that perhaps the house took over his life.

A BBC documentary about him, and the house, presented by Dan Cruickshank, can be bought from the online shop, as can Dennis Severs' book about his imagined Huguenots.

Evening visits are even more entrancing and mysterious, and the house is splendidly dressed for Christmas.

....

dennissevershouse.co.uk

18 Folgate Street, London E1 6BX

e: info@dennissevershouse.co.uk   t: 020 7247 4013

Open: Sun 12–4pm (last entry 3.15pm), Mon 12–2pm
(last entry 1.15pm); Silent Night – Mon, Wed & Fri 5–9pm (book
in advance); exclusive Silent Night once a month (more in Dec)
from 6pm – a two-hour visit with champagne/mulled wine and
mince pies (book in advance)

£10 / Silent Night £15 (£17.50 at Christmas) / exclusive Silent
Night from £50

Derwent Pencil Museum
Cumbria

The Pencil Museum is a standard entry on any list of strange or odd museums; along with the British Lawnmower Museum (see page 41), it's probably the granddaddy of them all, proud to announce that Keswick is 'the home of the pencil'. This may sound like hyperbole, but as you'll soon discover, it's nothing less than the truth.

The Lake District is very beautiful, but it does sometimes rain, as you'll know if you've ever been on holiday there. So any inside activity is always handy to know about. The Pencil Museum is more than a wet-weather diversion, however, and if you're an artist (or, indeed, a fan of stationery) it has the most wonderful shop full of beautiful art pencils and colouring books for children and adults. It's at the Derwent factory, where they've been making pencils since 1832.

Pencils are one of those things that seem so utterly ubiquitous that it's hard to imagine a time before they existed, but it wasn't until a graphite deposit was found at Seathwaite in the mid-16th century that there was anything, as it were, to put in them. (This is still the only deposit of graphite found in a form of sufficient solidity to be sawn into sticks.) It was thought to be a form of lead – which is why we refer to the stuff in pencils thus, even though it isn't.

For a long time, any graphite used for pencils had to be smuggled out of the mine; the mineral was used to line cannonball moulds, and the valuable deposit was claimed by the Crown. It's hard to imagine pencils as contraband, but maybe knowing this will make you think of them differently in future.

The softness of graphite is the reason for the wooden element of a pencil – as well as making a mess, naked graphite sticks would break too easily to be much use. Originally the sticks were wrapped in string for stability. No need for a sharpener – just unwind the wrapping.

England had a monopoly on the production of pencils until a way of reconstituting graphite powder was invented in Italy in the late 17th century. English pencils made with sticks sawn from natural graphite were made until the 1860s – traditionally these were square rather than cylindrical or hexagonal, which doesn't sound very comfortable for the user.

You enter the museum through a replica of the mine (and who doesn't like a replica mine?) Displays explain the history of the art of pencil making as well as describing the processes used today. The discovery of the graphite deposit resulted in a thriving cottage industry of pencil manufacture in Keswick, with mechanised processes developing during the 19th century. The Cumberland Pencil Company began in 1916, with colour pencils first being produced in 1932 (although they weren't non-toxic until the 1960s – so if you ever find a nice vintage set, don't chew them).

Most modern pencils are made from a mixture of graphite powder and clay – this process was developed during the Napoleonic Wars, as British graphite was no longer available to the French. The naval blockade meant no imports and left the French without access to pencils (*quelle horreur!*) until Nicolas-Jacques Conté's experiments with mixtures of clay and graphite, fired in a kiln, proved a success. Conté, of course, is still a very well-known manufacturer of pencils and pastels.

Back in Britain, sawn graphite was still used, and in 1838 Henry Bessemer, most famous for his invention of the Bessemer process for producing steel, also invented a method of compressing the powdered graphite waste from the pencil-sawing process, allowing it to be reused. (Did you know that the H in HB stands for 'hard' and the B for 'black' – harder pencils have more clay, darker ones more graphite.)

As well as pencil-making machinery and the famous 'giant pencil' – it's 26 feet long! It hangs from the ceiling! It's a prime photo opportunity! – they have some incredibly tiny and detailed 'pencil sculptures' where the leads (or, rather, the graphite) have been carved with remarkable precision, and some World War II pencils produced at the Cumberland factory under the Official Secrets Act. These conceal secret compasses and hidden maps and were issued to the aircrew of Lancaster bombers in case they ended up behind enemy lines. You can buy yourself a replica version in the shop – with a map of Keswick rather than anywhere further afield.

Many different kinds of art workshops for both children and adults are available (have a look at the website for more details), and there's also a coffee shop.

....

pencilmuseum.co.uk

Southey Works, Keswick, Cumbria CA12 5NG

t: 01768 773626

Open: Daily 9.30am–5pm (last entry 4pm); museum and shop closed for some of Dec (check website for details)

Adults – £4.95 / children – £3.95

Devil's Porridge Museum
Dumfries and Galloway

There's no debate about the fact that this place has the best name in the book. It's irresistible, isn't it? But what does it mean, you cry? Is it *actually* a porridge museum? Well, no. (Gap in the market?)

The 'porridge' in question is not oat-related and you probably shouldn't: a) heat it up; or b) poke it with a spurtle. This museum explores the history of HM Factory Gretna, which, during World War I, was the world's biggest munitions factory. It also tells the story of the Solway Coast during World War II.

The 'devil's porridge' is the name given to the explosive slurry (actually a type of cordite) produced by the thousands of women, known as 'Gretna Girls', who were brought up here for their war work. The name itself was coined by none other than Sir Arthur Conan Doyle, who came on a visit to write it up for the papers.

Although it started life in a church before moving to an unheated shed, the museum now lives in a very stylish, purpose-built modern building, and there's a cafe too. It's beautifully and thoughtfully arranged, and the displays are fascinating, with plenty of original artefacts as well as some wonderful archive photography. You can see uniforms, medals and machinery, and outside there's the Barclay fireless locomotive, *Sir James*, recently repainted with camouflage paint, which was one of 34 engines that used to move stuff round the huge site. (The immense factory site stretched for 9 miles, from Longtown in Cumbria to Eastriggs, and had its own transport network – including 125 miles of narrow-gauge track and an independent water supply – as well as a coal-fired power station providing electricity, two townships for the workers, and the four sites that actually produced the munitions.)

As well as information about the manufacturing process, there are room settings to help you imagine what life was like for the Gretna Girls and the rest of the 30,000 staff who lived and worked there. The entire factory site was constructed between August 1915 and April 1916, built by 10,000 (mostly Irish) navvies.

All this frantic activity took place because of the so-called 'Shell Crisis' – a significant and worrying lack of ammunition for the British Army in France. David Lloyd George was appointed Minister of Munitions and HM Factory Gretna was the result of his project to significantly improve the situation. By April 1916, hundreds of engineers, chemists and explosive experts had been recruited, as well as the 12,000 women needed to work on the production lines, which included mixing waste cotton and nitric acid in the large stoneware basins – or Thomson nitrating pans – to make the 'devil's porridge' itself, one of the first stages in the production of cordite propellant. You can see examples of the pans at the museum to get an idea of the scale of this task.

Other exhibits cover the wide range of activity on the Solway Coast during World War II. The area saw a further influx of people, from evacuees and POWs to workers at the ammunition depots run by the Ministry of Supply on the site of the former HM Factory Gretna. Munitions were still produced in the area, in factories run by ICI. The nearby RAF Annan was home to fighter pilots during training, and after the war it became the site of Scotland's first nuclear power station. You can learn more about post-war developments such as the Cold War and nuclear power in Scotland, and experience a VR (virtual reality) headset-enabled exploration of the Chapelcross nuclear power station. This new technology allows access to high-security areas, including the turbine hall, the reactor control room and the pile cap, where the nuclear fuel rods were installed – as well as the top-secret tritium plant, where the fuel for British hydrogen bombs was processed.

There are lots of costumes to try on, including a gas mask if you fancy it, and there's quite a lot of interactivity, so this is a great museum for children. There are also frequent talks and activities – it's well worth checking the website for details.

devilsporridge.org.uk

Stanfield, Annan Road, Eastriggs, Dumfries and Galloway, Scotland DG12 6TF

t: 01461 700021

Open: Mon–Sat 10am–5pm; Sun 10am–4pm; closed over Christmas (check website for details)

Adults – £6 / children 5 to 16 – £5

Dog Collar Museum
Kent

Before you gasp at astonishment at the ticket price, be reassured – this isn't just for the dog collars but for the whole of the enormous Leeds Castle estate, from the fantastically photogenic castle itself, parts of which date back 900 years (it was owned by six medieval queens), to the stunning gardens and some really top-level adventure playgrounds for the kids.

There's a maze, an impressive shell grotto and frequent falconry displays at the Bird of Prey Centre. For an additional (small) fee you can get a ferry across the lake (known as the Great Water) or go for a punt on the moat. Plus there's a Go Ape! Tree Top Adventure, and if you're feeling extravagant you can take a Segway tour through the grounds. At any rate, whatever you decide to do during your visit, there's a *lot* to see at Leeds Castle and you might be feeling weary by the time you reach the stable courtyard that's home to the Dog Collar Museum. It's an add-on, an

extra, you might feel – perhaps
it's time for a coffee or to
drag the picnic from the
car. You'd be missing
out, though, if you
neglected this element
of the experience.
And it's very small,
so you needn't worry
that it will take hours to
walk round it – more like
15 minutes.

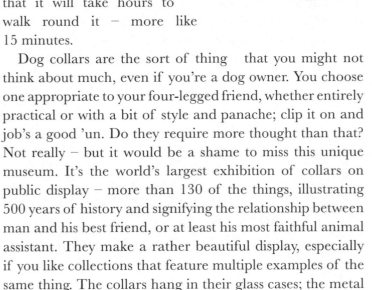

Dog collars are the sort of thing   that you might not
think about much, even if you're a dog owner. You choose
one appropriate to your four-legged friend, whether entirely
practical or with a bit of style and panache; clip it on and
job's a good 'un. Do they require more thought than that?
Not really – but it would be a shame to miss this unique
museum. It's the world's largest exhibition of collars on
public display – more than 130 of the things, illustrating
500 years of history and signifying the relationship between
man and his best friend, or at least his most faithful animal
assistant. They make a rather beautiful display, especially
if you like collections that feature multiple examples of the
same thing. The collars hang in their glass cases; the metal
ones, sparkling in silver and silver gilt as well as more
quotidian steel, resemble particularly chunky bracelets.
Of course, it's best not to think about how all the dogs
for whom they were made are long dead, or you may feel
unexpectedly melancholic.

Anyway, there are some very elegant collars for exotic
lapdogs and the dogs of royalty and nobility, and much

more practical ones for working dogs, including some rather terrifyingly spiked examples like the earliest one in the collection. Dating from the late 15th century, it's made from iron and designed for a Spanish herd mastiff, intended to protect it from bears and wolves. There are also some hefty leather and brass ones.

You can quite clearly see the progression from 'My dog is extremely tough' to 'My dog is extremely valuable and luxurious' as the collars get fancier from the 18th century onwards, looking in some cases like the sort of items the dogs' owners might wear themselves. Many are decorated with engravings, not just of the dog's name but the owner's too, their address in case the dog got lost, and perhaps the owner's crest or coat of arms – maybe even some poetry. The metal ones are hinged, sometimes in more than one place, with clasps to fasten them, and sometimes they're lined with leather or velvet. There are modern collars too, made from all different materials – beads, plastic, and even old tyres.

More than 60 of the collars were collected by historian John Hunt and his wife, Gertrude, who donated them to the museum in 1977. Both were avid collectors of art and antiques, the dog collars the most unusual and perhaps unexpected part of their collection. Since that first donation, many more have been given by the public as well as being purchased by the museum. Following the revamp of the collection, 30 more collars, discovered in storage, have been displayed for the first time.

....

leeds-castle.com/attractions

Leeds Castle, Maidstone, Kent ME17 1PL

For sat nav use ME17 1RG

e: enquiries@leeds-castle.co.uk   t: 01622 765400

Open: Apr–Sep daily – grounds 10am–6pm,
castle 10.30am–5.30pm

Oct–Mar daily – grounds 10am–5pm, castle 10.30am–4pm

Adults – £26 / children 4 to 15 – £17.50 / children under 4 –
free (tickets are for a year's access)

Dunrobin Castle Museum
Sutherland

The other places in this book that have a lot of taxidermy are generally natural history museums or piecemeal collections by people who like taxidermy. The museum at Dunrobin is a bit different.

The animals that greet you on arrival aren't the victims of science or curiosity, but of people who just, you know, liked shooting things. It's hard to get your head round this, really. Also it reminds you that quite a lot of the taxidermy that you see outside natural history museums is of native British mammals – foxes, badgers, squirrels; all quite common, whatever you think about killing them – or types of deer and antelope that, even now, tend to live in herds and which, therefore, there might be lots of. Here, though, we have things 'bagged on safari', and seeing a giraffe and bits of elephant or rhino really does make you think about a time when this wasn't just acceptable but encouraged. Especially if you were rich, of course, and the Dukes of Sutherland weren't short of a bob or two. Sailing to Africa to shoot things was a regular occurrence. The sign outside warning you about what you're going to see is a sensible precaution; it is quite shocking, however beautifully prepared and mounted the animals are. There's more to it than the sad eyes of death, however. It's a fine example of a private museum, and demonstrates that the Sutherlands were interested in pretty much everything, even if there's a caveat of 'as long as we can own it'.

The castle itself is well worth a visit. It's one of Britain's oldest continuously inhabited houses, dating back in parts to the early 1300s. It has a rather unnecessary 189 rooms, and looks like a fairytale French château. Home to the Earls and later the Dukes of Sutherland, it stands high on a terrace above spectacular formal gardens, with fantastic views across the Moray Firth and the North Sea.

The museum is housed in a fine 18th-century building in the gardens. Built in 1762 by William, 16th Earl of Sutherland, as a summer house, it was extended by the 3rd Duke, specifically to provide a suitable place in which to display the large collection of objects brought back by the family from all over the world. The 4th and 5th Dukes were the ones who really went to town with it though. First up are the hunting trophies, but if you can get though this there's loads of other stuff to see. Upstairs is the ethnographic/anthropological collection, mostly also collected in Africa, with lots of weapons and beadwork, as well as items like Inuit fishing equipment, from travels elsewhere. Downstairs, at the back, displayed in beautifully constructed glass-fronted cabinets or hanging from the walls, and lit by a splendid roof-light that allows lots of natural light in to a room that would otherwise be rather dark, there are lots of mounted antlers, birds' eggs, geological specimens and a fine collection of archaeological exhibits, many discovered on land belonging to the Sutherlands. There's a fine display of carved Pictish symbol stones and prehistoric ceramics, stone axes and so on. In addition, you can see a slipper that belonged to Garibaldi and look in awe at a handkerchief of Queen Victoria's. Everything is laid out as it was in the late-19th to early 20th century, so in many ways it's a museum of how museums used to be.

....

Dunrobin Castle, Golspie, Sutherland KW10 6SF

t: 01408 633177

Open: Apr–May & Oct daily 10.30am–4.30pm, Jun–Sep daily 10am–5pm. Last entry half an hour before closing time. Museum open 11am–4pm

Admission included in Castle ticket price (Adults – £12/ children – £7.50)

Fan Museum

London

There's lots to see in Greenwich, which is much prettier than you might remember. If you're tired of tunnels beneath the Thames and all things maritime, then it's just a short walk from the DLR station at Greenwich Cutty Sark to Crooms Hill.

The Fan Museum is found in two appropriately charming and elegant 18th-century houses, beautifully renovated as a home for Hélène Alexander's astonishingly comprehensive collection. Downstairs, you can watch an introductory film in a room filled with cases containing fans from all over the world. These illustrate the history of the fan, with examples dating back several centuries, and will allow you to familiarise yourself with the correct terminology of sticks, risers and pivots, and with the development of this most practical and beautiful of objects. Fixed fans (ones that don't fold up) have a history stretching back at least 5,000 years.

This room and the other on the ground floor, which displays unmounted fan art (including pieces by Walter Sickert and Paul Gauguin), form the permanent collection, while upstairs the exhibition changes regularly. During a September 2018 visit it was 'The Romantic Age – European Fans 1810–1840', making the most of the museum's huge collection of early 19th-century fans, as well as other objects that would have belonged to the fans' owners, including manicure sets and notebooks and a rather splendid travelling coffee set.

Particularly pleasing examples include fans designed for you to write your dance partners' names on during a ball, so you don't embarrassingly double-book any dances, and one featuring Zarafa, the giraffe presented to the King of France in 1827. She was the first giraffe seen in Europe for three centuries and everyone was understandably thrilled. She became immensely famous and popular and could be found as a motif on all sorts of objects.

The earliest fans are known only from pictorial sources, and it's thought they date (in terms of something specifically manufactured, rather than a useful leaf picked up for the purpose) from at least 3000BC. Early fans were all of the fixed type – the folding fan wasn't invented until relatively recently. It seems such an obvious idea now, but just think about how amazed you'd be the first time you ever saw one.

Fixed fans known as 'flabella' were used by the church as liturgical objects during the early medieval period; they were intended to keep insects away from the Host. The development of the fan in Europe was influenced by developments in China, Japan and Korea, with new designs travelling along the Spice Routes. The first

European folding fans were copied from prototypes that arrived with merchants from the Far East and were pretty much only made in very expensive materials. This restricted their use to royalty and the nobility, who could afford the ivory or mother-of-pearl and tortoiseshell the sticks and guards were made from. Gradually, a market developed and guilds like the Worshipful Company of Fan Makers were formed for the craftsmen who made them. From the 17th century, fans can be seen in portraits of society ladies, as they became not just fashionable but an essential part of one's costume. Feather fans were the usual style in the early years of the century but folding fans eventually made those look completely passé, fit only for the aspiring middle classes. How dreadful!

In the 18th century, fans were imported in increasing quantities from the Far East, generally by the Dutch and English East India Companies. Printed fans were also developed – these were obviously much cheaper than hand-painted ones, bringing the folding fan well within the grasp of a much wider audience. Where once fans had been adorned with graceful classical imagery, by the beginning of the 19th century you might have preferred something a bit more contemporary – perhaps a subject like 'How to Play Whist and not lose your Temper!' Early 19th-century fans were smaller, with more attention paid to the decoration of the sticks, and brisé fans became very popular. (These are fans where all the sticks are exposed, and often intricately pierced.) Fans got larger and more lavish as the 19th century progressed, with well-known artists painting fan leaves, and unknown artists who painted fan leaves becoming quite famous.

The 20th century saw advertising featuring on fans, and extravagant ostrich-feather versions becoming all the rage. While never as fashionable as they had once been, fans continued to be manufactured and used, often bought as souvenirs or commemorative items. Extremely desirable *haute couture* fans are still made in France today.

The collection at the Fan Museum is surely one of the most exhaustive anywhere, with fans from the 11th century onwards. By the time you've worked your way round everything on display, you'll wonder if there can possibly be a design that you haven't seen. If you're at the museum on one of the days when the Orangery is open for tea, you'll need a reviving pot of something and perhaps a scone. You'll also wonder if there's a practical way to get more fans into your own life – or perhaps you'll be thinking smugly of the one you always carry just in case things get overheated on the Tube.

....

thefanmuseum.org.uk

12 Crooms Hill, Greenwich, London SE10 8ER

e: info@thefanmuseum.org.uk
t: 020 8305 1441

Open: Feb–Dec Tue–Sat 11am–5pm,
Sun 12–5pm

Adults – £5 / children – £3

Afternoon tea in
the Orangery: Tue,
Fri–Sun, 12.30–4.30pm
(last sitting 4pm)

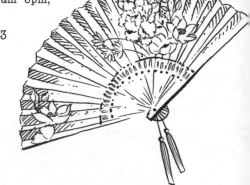

Freud Museum
London

*Sigmund Freud shaped the twentieth century idea of what
a person is; we would not recognise ourselves without him.*
Marina Warner

**Not so much 'weird', perhaps, but very specific,
and the only museum in this book dedicated to
a particular person (or people – it's not all about
Sigmund, you know).**

Although both less controversial and less popular than it
once was, psychoanalysis is still hugely influential, having
an ongoing impact within the humanities as well as in
psychotherapy, psychiatry and psychology – and Freud is
still a giant presence in the field. References to his work
and theories can be seen in pretty much every aspect of
contemporary popular culture. Anyone with an interest
in the development of the talking therapies, or in 20th-
century social history, will find the museum a fascinating

place to visit. Our continued exposure to Freud's ideas through late 20th-century and early 21st-century popular culture makes it quite difficult to fully grasp how dangerous and controversial his ideas were when he first began to explore and discuss them. His views undermined all kinds of cultural values and a lot of reactions to them were very hostile.

The Freuds left their home in Vienna in 1938 after Austria was annexed by the Nazis. They escaped thanks to significant financial support from their friends, in particular Princess Marie Bonaparte (Napoleon's great-grandniece – her husband, Prince George of Greece and Denmark, was Prince Philip's uncle, so it's fair to say she had useful connections) who helped raise the money for the 'flight tax' imposed on Jewish citizens who wished to leave countries under German control (about £150,000 in today's money). Four of Freud's sisters remained in Austria and died as a result of the Holocaust.

After arriving in London, Freud, his wife Martha and their daughter Anna eventually moved into this beautiful red-brick house, with its impressively large windows and pretty garden, which had been remodelled in part by their son Ernst, an architect. Sigmund was already very well known, of course, for his pioneering work as the founder of psychoanalysis, and his daughter Anna was also already working as a child psychoanalyst.

This was the Freuds' home and is full of their furniture and belongings. You can see Sigmund's famous couch, where his patients lay and discussed their thoughts and feelings, as well as a large collection of objects, including his library (he was able to bring only some of it with him from Austria – around a third of his books had to be sold) and the many antiquities he kept around him in his study. There are personal items, too – his pen, his glasses, his boots – which seem rather ordinary in contrast to the multitudes of bronze and terracotta statuettes, Buddhas, ancient Greek pots and Roman and Egyptian artefacts. If you have studied Freud and his work, there are a number of items that you will have read about, and visitors are often surprised at their reactions to things like the couch and the art produced by Freud's patients. His study remains almost exactly as it was when he lived here, as does Anna Freud's own study, complete with typewriter and her own books, *objets d'art* and (less famous) couch.

The museum is also home to an extensive archive of photographs and personal documents, including letters and press cuttings, and on the landing you'll see two portraits of Freud – one by Ferdinand Schmutzer, the other by Salvador Dalí, who visited Freud here in London. Also on display are two paintings by Sergei Pankejeff, one of Freud's most famous patients. The paintings depict the childhood nightmare he recounted to Freud, which earned him the nickname 'Wolf Man'.

Freud didn't begin his career as a psychoanalyst – such a thing didn't exist. He studied physiology, anatomy, botany, chemistry and physics, hoping to become a natural scientist like Darwin, whom he greatly admired. He became an expert in neuroanatomy and published several studies of the nervous systems of fish, as well as writing books on language disorders (aphasia) and childhood cerebral palsy, and researching and publishing on the anaesthetic properties of cocaine. (There's the anaesthesia theme again.) He had to give up all this research when he got married, as he needed a steady income.

In 1886, after training as a doctor, he set up in practice, specialising in nervous disorders. An interest in hypnotism, which he developed during his training, made him wonder if sometimes physical symptoms could have a psychological cause, and if hypnotism could help him access the traumatic memories suppressed by his patients that might be causing their symptoms.

After a while he gave up the hypnosis, merely asking his patients to 'free associate' – to say whatever came to mind, no matter how silly or unpleasant it might seem. Free association is, of course, the basis of psychoanalysis, with the tiniest and apparently most unimportant thoughts and memories leading to the central longings and urges of the person being analysed. He theorised about the dynamic unconscious, where all the things we try hard not to think about exist, and which leads us to accidentally express these things through dreams and slips of the tongue (Freudian slips). Most famously, perhaps, he explored the complexity of sibling, parent/child and other familial relationships. The events of childhood have an intense and life-long impact on our thoughts and emotions, and he was one of the first people to explore this, leading to revolutionary ideas about sexuality and theories about the libido, the ego and the id.

A useful audio guide is available if you want it, and the shop sells lots of quirky Freud-themed items (Freudian slippers, anyone?) – it's a good place to buy unusual gifts, ideal for anyone you know who is a psychoanalyst, or sees one, or is just interested in the workings of the mind. The detailed guide to the objects on Freud's desk is particularly fascinating. Each one is significant and meaningful, with its own story, and the book explores them in detail.

There are regular temporary exhibitions, and events take place throughout the year, from talks given by the curators on specific aspects of the house or collection to courses covering elements of psychoanalysis and film screenings followed by discussions. Have a look at the website to see what's on.

....

freud.org.uk
20 Maresfield Gardens, London NW3 5SX
e: info@freud.org.uk   t: 020 7435 2002
Open: Wed–Sun 12–5pm
Adults – £9 / children 12 to 16 – £5 / children under 12 – free

Gem Rock Museum
Dumfries and Galloway

This is not an area exactly stuffed full of tourist attractions, so you'll see plenty of signs for the Gem Rock Museum and it comes up in all the lists of places to visit.

Scotland can sometimes be the sort of place where indoor activities are useful things to have up your sleeve, but it would be a shame to miss this place just because you've been lucky with the weather. There are lots of sparkly and shiny things to look at, including an actual gold nugget (one of the largest on display in the UK) and a rather fabulous set of replicas of the world's largest diamonds. It's fun and interesting (if maybe a little old-fashioned) and they have very friendly staff, a large cafe and free wi-fi.

The museum is housed in an old school and the collection includes examples of crystals and gemstones found in Britain as well as around the world. They also have a good collection of fossils, including a fossilised egg, the skeleton of a Russian bear, and a meteorite that is 4.5 billion years old. There's a replica of the Welcome Stranger, the biggest gold nugget ever found, which weighed more than 69kg – its discovery (in 1869) must have seriously improved the day of the men who found it.

Make sure you check out the Crystal Cave – it claims to be a 'realistic cave setting', which may be pushing it a bit, but it's fun nonetheless. There are some excellent examples in here anyway, including some very large quartz crystals and fine amethyst geodes. The best bit is the fluorescent display, which is genuinely quite extraordinary – watch as the apparently dull specimens glow in a very unnatural fashion under the ultraviolet light. It is completely natural, though, all caused by the composition of the minerals.

The cases in the museum's main room contain various gems and crystals grouped together, so if you're a particular fan of tiger's eye, for example, or onyx, you'll have your own favourite cabinet. Some of the gems are in their raw form, while others are cut and polished into balls, egg shapes or various kinds of jewellery or ornaments, some antique or unusual. Pretty much everything is labelled with its country of origin as well as its name, so you know what you're looking at.

You might wonder what differentiates 'any old rock' from the rocks that make a proper effort and form crystals. Well, all rocks are minerals, but not all minerals are rocks. The commonest minerals – things like feldspars, quartz, mica and calcite – come together in various combinations to form most types of rock. There are more than 3,000 types of minerals, but generally you don't get enough of these in any location for them to be considered 'rock forming'. So that's the very basic explanation, and from here things get a bit more scientific – you may remember some of this stuff from chemistry lessons. Minerals themselves are composed of elements (which, as you'll recall, are substances that can't be broken down any further and are the chaps you find in the Periodic Table).

Many minerals are made up of lots of different elements and their formulas are complex. Given the right circumstances, minerals will form into crystals, the shape of which is determined by the mineral's internal atomic structure. The way they grow is affected by many things – temperature, pressure, how much room there is available, and whether they form from solutions (did you grow copper sulphate crystals at school?) or during volcanic eruptions.

People have valued minerals for thousands of years and for a variety of reasons – you can use graphite to draw (see the Derwent Pencil Museum, page 72) or as a lubricant, and ochre to paint (see Clearwell Caves, page 58). You can burn coal and use tin and copper to make bronze. You can make a lovely pair of earrings from diamonds, and fill the holes in your teeth with gold (actually, it's probably easier for someone else to do this rather than trying to do it yourself). Many minerals have practical uses, but others are valued for their rarity or beauty.

The colour of a mineral is one of the things that make it interesting – and one of the reasons why the Gem Rock Museum doesn't just have cases full of grey rocks. The differences in colour and form are what makes them attractive to the collector. The colours we see are visible to us because of the way our brains and eyes interpret light waves, and the different ways the crystals absorb and reflect the light. Some minerals will appear as different colours depending on what's going on with their internal structure and whether they contain impurities. These are known as 'allochromatic', and that's why you sometimes get pink (or black or green) diamonds, or the various colours of quartz, like purple amethyst, or citrine, which can vary from pale lemon yellow to brown.

Others contain light-absorbing atoms as part of their structure and are almost always the same colour. These are known as 'idiochromatic' minerals – malachite is a good example, as it's always more or less the same startling swirly green colour.

The minerals most likely to affect the colour of a gem or crystal are copper, iron, manganese, titanium and chromium. Interestingly, chromium can produce the green of an emerald or the red of a ruby. Garnets are also red, but their colour comes from iron, which also gives sapphires their blue, although the best ones also contain titanium. Confused? There's certainly a lot to learn about minerals.

So what makes a mineral a 'gem'? Gemstones are usually crystals, and to qualify they have to have certain properties relating to clarity, colour and hardness. The rarer and more beautiful they are, the more value they have to collectors. More than 200 stones are recognised as gemstones, with some minerals giving us more than one type of gem depending on which impurity or combination of impurities they contain.

As well as the displays of minerals, the museum has a Victorian-themed study with comfortable sofas, lots of books, and an audiovisual presentation explaining how various minerals were formed. The shop is, as you might expect, heavy on the gemstone jewellery. It's not just jewellery, either – there's a very wide selection of gifts of the crystal/rock/gem/fossil variety. Some good science-based stuff for the kids, too, including grow-your-own crystal kits.

....

gemrock.net

Chain Road, Creetown, Dumfries and Galloway, Scotland DG8 7HJ

e: enquiries@gemrock.net   t: 01671 820357

Open: Feb–Mar Wed–Sun 10am–4pm; Apr–Sep daily 9.30am–5.30pm; Oct daily 10am–4pm; Nov–22 Dec Wed–Sun 10am–4pm; closed 23 Dec–31 Jan (last entry half an hour before closing)

Adults – £5 / children 5 to 15 – £3 / children under 5 – free (tickets valid for two weeks)

Grant Museum of Zoology
London

You may scoff at the notion that a natural history museum could be considered 'weird'. However strange the twists and turns of the natural world, you may say, its strangeness comes only from unfamiliarity.

True enough, and yet anyone who's ever watched a nature programme will know the natural world is full of weirdness, from the kangaroo's three vaginas to the corkscrew egg cases of the bullhead shark. And this is a place where you can expect to find all kinds of curious and intriguing natural wonders. Did you know that around 95% of known animal species are smaller than a human thumb? This is a good place to look at some of them.

The Grant Museum is 'the last university natural history museum in London', left over from a time when there were similar assemblages at every university worth its salt. The majority of the exhibits were collected for research purposes by endless streams of Victorian naturalists, trampling desert and jungle to bring back examples of various species in order that someone in a draughty room lit by gas lamps could dissect them, give them a name and decide where they fitted on the spreading branches of the tree of life.

If you like skeletons and preserved specimens – and, let's face it, why wouldn't you? – this is a treasure house of bone and tissue. The museum has more than 68,000 specimens, from the tiniest teeth and organs to the skeletons of elephants and whales. It's also a wonderful archive of handwritten labels: the backlit space (like a science lift!) known as the micrarium is filled with endless microscope slides that stretch above your head, each tiny slither neatly labelled in a variety of handwriting. It's probably enough to make a visit worthwhile on its own. There are more than 20,000 microscope slides in the collection, and 2,323 of them are displayed here – slices of plants and eyeballs, preserved spiders, fleas, blood vessels, molluscs and tiny cells of all kinds. And have a look for the mammoth's hair.

Specimens of extinct animals are always interesting – they have some dodo bones, the skeleton of a quagga (a kind of zebra) and several thylacine specimens. If you think the dodo's story is depressing, the thylacine's is worse. An example of convergent evolution, they were the marsupial equivalent of the dog, although usually described as 'wolves' or 'Tasmanian tigers'. They were hunted to extinction in the 1930s due to a combination of bad press (alleged sheep-killing) and lack of interest in their preservation. Unbelievably, no study was made of these creatures in the wild and the last one died of neglect in a zoo in Hobart, Tasmania in 1936.

But what of the museum's own history? When Robert Edmond Grant (1793–1874) arrived at the newly founded

University of London (later University College London) in 1827 as the first Professor of Zoology and Comparative Anatomy in England, he was unimpressed to discover that there were no teaching materials available. He immediately began to amass the specimens, diagrams, lecture notes and material for dissection that form the basis of the museum today. When he died, he left them his library and a collection of specimens already in the tens of thousands. His own work concentrated on marine invertebrates, particularly sponges – he was the person who finally proved that they were animals, not plants, and he was a big influence on Charles Darwin. The collection has been in continuous use by students at the university since 1828, and first opened to the public in 1996.

Some of the specimens have been acquired from various former university collections; they also have material from London Zoo and the comparative anatomy collections of a number of London hospitals. There's material from the Discovery and Challenger expeditions, and other things to look out for include the Blaschka glass models of invertebrates. Stunningly beautiful, anatomically perfect models of creatures that were hard to preserve, like sea anemones and jellyfish, they were made in the late 19th century by Leopold and Rudolph Blaschka, Czech jewellers. No one's entirely sure how they were made, and the process has never been replicated.

The brain collection is a comparative anatomy collection, showing the differences between the brains of various mammals (and a turtle). The brains hang in their jars, preserved in alcohol, and some have been dissected to show their internal structure. If you like that, you'll love the Negus collection of bisected heads. Sir Victor Negus, who was a laryngologist, prepared the collection to research the larynxes of various species. You can see a pangolin, a wallaby, a chimp and a sloth, among others. If you've ever seen Damien Hirst's bisected cow and calf, *Mother and Child (Divided)*, these specimens will seem familiar – the perfect 'face' of the animal on one side, the complex interior workings on the other.

The museum's website is excellent, their jar of moles has its own Twitter account (@GlassJarofMoles), and they have frequent events and temporary exhibitions. As it's still part of the university, PhD students are often available to answer questions and tell you more about various exhibits. It really is a wonderful place, full of the quirkily fascinating and irreplaceable.

....

ucl.ac.uk/culture/grant-museum-zoology

Rockefeller Building, University College London, 21 University Street, London WC1E 6DE

Open: Mon–Sat 1–5pm; closed Christmas & Easter

Free

High Wycombe Chair-making Museum

Buckinghamshire

Where would you get a chair before IKEA and Oak Furnitureland existed? Once upon a time, those of us who couldn't afford fancy bespoke furniture would have made them ourselves, or bought a variety of locally made, vernacular items. Gradually one area of England began to dominate the chair trade. The beech woods of Buckinghamshire were the ideal place to find the wood and make the legs and stretchers of common types of chair like the Windsor – now a standard item in many antique shops at prices that would startle the people who made them.

They've been making chairs here since before 1700, with the trade developing rapidly in the 19th century in response to equally rapid population growth, particularly in London but also throughout the rest of the country. As the market for chairs grew, so High Wycombe became famous for producing them. Very large commissions were regularly taken. In 1873 an order for 19,200 chairs for an evangelical meeting was completed in a few weeks.

The legs and stretchers were made by itinerant craftsmen, known since the early 20th century as 'bodgers'. They worked with green, unseasoned wood, buying a stand of trees and often living right there in the woods in roughly made lean-to huts. They used pole lathes to turn the wood, also made on site. It was a semi-industrialised business, with the legs and stretchers being made in bulk and sold on to the people who took on the next step. The amount made in High Wycombe and the surrounding area was so high – by 1875 it was estimated they were making an astonishing 4,700 chairs a day – that other regional chair-producing centres in the Cotswolds and the northwest were pretty much completely wiped out.

Three types of craftsmen were required for chair manufacture. In addition to the bodger there was the 'benchman', who was more likely to work in a workshop in a town or village, and who made the sawn parts – the seat, and in some cases the back. Then the 'framer' put the whole thing together. The bodgers worked fast. They could produce around a gross of parts a day – that's 144 pieces – cutting up the wood, making it into blanks, then turning it.

Eventually it wasn't just chairs that were produced here, with a number of furniture companies moving out from London, including what would eventually become Parker Knoll. Production increased after both World Wars and by the 1950s Parker Knoll, Ercol and G-Plan furniture was all produced here. In 1960 there were still more than 100 furniture companies in the area, although by the 1990s this was much reduced and the recession of the early 90s saw the closure of the G-Plan factory. Ercol moved elsewhere and even Parker Knoll stopped production in High Wycombe. Smaller factories remain, however, and furniture is still made in the town.

(The official mascot of Wycombe Wanderers FC – nicknamed 'The Chairboys' – is called 'Bodger', named after the team's record goalscorer, Tony Horseman, who played for the town 1961–78. He had worked in the furniture industry, although never as an actual bodger.)

The museum itself is tiny – just one room of chairs and tools – but like a lot of the places in this book, the enthusiasm shown by the owner is infectious. The little tour is fascinating, and you'll see demonstrations of wood-turning using original tools like the shave horse, pole and treadle lathes, as well as learning about various types of locally made chairs.

Don't miss the upstairs gallery, which has paintings for sale as well as turned wood bowls and other items.

....

kraftinwood.com

Kraftinwood, Kraft Village, Grafton Street, High Wycombe, Buckinghamshire HP12 3AJ

t: 01494 533302

Open: Mon–Wed, Fri–Sat 9–5, Sun 12–5

£4

Please note that the brown tourist signs directing visitors to the museum lead to the old museum site, so don't follow them!

Hollycombe Steam in the Country

Hampshire

Who doesn't like a steam railway and a proper, beautiful roundabout (more on the name later...) with galloping horses?

Even if you're too young to remember steam engines, like certain other things you've never experienced directly – the sound of a Spitfire, for example – the smell of traction engines and the music of a calliope are very evocative. And if you, or your kids, have never experienced these things, this is the ideal place to fix that.

Hollycombe is a Hampshire country estate, with beautiful gardens begun in the late 19th century. More than a million trees were planted from the 1880s onwards, and the Azalea Walk dates from the mid-1920s. The gardens look wonderful all year, with magnolias and bluebells making a particularly good show in the spring, and very fine autumn colours. There's an ice house and a 'Romantic

View' – something we should all have, surely. But lovely as the gardens are, it's really all about the steam. And there's more to see here than just a little railway or a roundabout.

For most people, perhaps, the idea of the history of machinery in farming goes from horse power to the internal combustion engine without a pause, but on larger farms, steam power was used in a variety of perhaps surprising ways. 'Barn machinery' – mostly devices used to prepare feed for animals – can be seen here, run by a horizontal steam engine, although this is generally a static display. (Local visitors might be interested to know that this engine spent some of its life driving a well pump at Basing House.) Big estates might also have used steam power for sawmills, and beam engines (an early form of steam engine) were often used to run threshing machines and mills, sometimes with a bewildering number of belts running different machinery. The beam engine at Hollycombe dates from 1850 and runs regularly on open Sundays – check the website if you want to see it running.

They have some 'road steam' as well – a couple of steamrollers, one built locally in 1932. The other one, *David*, dates from 1921 and worked for Islington Borough Council until 1955. Then there's the miniature Garden Railway, which you might think is just for children but can easily manage a train full of grown-ups. It travels from a station near the sawmill in a loop through the gardens, and the journey takes about five minutes. If you fancy something a bit bigger, the narrow-gauge Quarry Railway has a couple of steam locomotives and also a diesel. The carriages were originally used by Ramsgate's electric Tunnel Railway (one has a wheelchair compartment),

and the track runs through the woods and fields for about a mile and a half to the old quarry. There are lovely views of the South Downs and Sussex Weald.

So that's already lots of steam. And although it's all interesting, and the railways are fun, there's no denying that probably the most popular exhibits are the splendid steam-driven Victorian and Edwardian fairground rides. This is surely the largest collection of working steam fairground rides in the country, and it includes the world's first white-knuckle ride, the Razzle Dazzle. It's the only surviving example and dates from 1906. It was the first ride with a rotational *and* tilting motion – so hang on tight.

Mr Field's Steam Circus is an early forerunner of the 'gallopers' and dates to the 1870s or thereabouts; it's the oldest surviving mechanically driven fairground ride. The horses just go round, rather than going up and down at the same time as they do on a standard roundabout. Some people may find this preferable. It was restored in 2015 but doesn't run all the time – only on special occasions.

Did you know that, although roundabouts are also called merry-go-rounds, and carousels in the US and Europe, technically those run in the opposite direction? British roundabouts run clockwise, while the others go anti-clockwise – which is surely all kinds of wrong. Impress your friends by identifying the nationality of any roundabout with ease.

The roundabout at Hollycombe is of the 'three-abreast steam gallopers' type, and was built in 1912. As well as the 24 beautifully painted horses, it has six cockerels and two chariots (ideal if the galloping motion makes you feel queasy). If that's not enough excitement for you there's the steam-driven chair-o-planes – a ride that has had a very exciting life. It started out in 1910 as a roundabout with horses, but while it was in storage during World War II it was partially destroyed by an incendiary bomb and consequently converted to chair-o-planes. It might be the only steam-driven example of this ride ever created.

In addition to this, though rather calmer and more relaxing, there are steam-powered swing boats dating from 1901. You get to control how high your boat swings by pulling a rope. Then, once you've exhausted the thrill of the fair, you can stagger into the bioscope for some cinematic relaxation. Bioscopes were also travelling entertainment, like the fairground rides, with a steam engine generating electricity for the projector and lights.

In September and October the fairground is open for business on Saturday evenings for a real taste of old-fashioned entertainment.

------

hollycombe.co.uk
Iron Hill, Liphook, Hampshire GU30 7LP
e: info@hollycombe.co.uk   t: 01428 724900

Open: Various days from 11am with rides from 12.30pm (last entry 4pm); Sep–Oct Sat 7–10pm (check the website for open days); closed in winter

Adults – £17 / children 3 to 15 – £14

Ice House at the
London Canal Museum

London

A couple of streets east of King's Cross Station you'll find the London Canal Museum. Regent's Canal runs to the north of the station, adding to the charming ambience of Granary Square and giving the employees of the *Guardian* something to look at while they eat their lunch.

Canals are funny places; it's always odd to see something built for a busy industrial purpose transformed into a view and a leisure activity. It's still busy round here, of course, still noisy, and crowded in places, but no one is unloading great cargoes of coal or nails or timber, there are no horses, and the people who live on the narrow boats don't (generally) travel the country in them. Anyway, the London Canal Museum tells the story of London's canals and it's an interesting one. It's a well-laid-out little museum with lots of great exhibits, including a partial barge you can explore, and access to the actual canal basin.

But that's not why we're here – canals are not 'weird' or unusual in any sense, are they? There are other canal museums. This one's different because it's housed in a building with a secret. The high arched entrance to the museum was built to allow access for the horses and carts that came here to collect ice, of all things. In the 19th and early 20th centuries, most of the ice consumed in London – whether keeping bottles of champagne chilled in fancy hotels, or assisting in the creation of ice cream, or being dropped into gassy mineral water or glasses of whisky – came from Norway, imported by ship from the frozen lakes of the snowy north. The Norwegians exported their ice to India and Australia, too, which seems incredible. But we're not concerned with that. We're concerned with the ice that arrived here at Battlebridge Basin by barge, and was unloaded at Gatti's ice warehouse and packed neatly into the two immense circular pits or caverns excavated beneath the ground, dug from the London clay.

Carlo Gatti (1817–78) was a Swiss-Italian, and he came to London in 1847. His ambition was to make his fortune – an ambition fully realised, as he died a millionaire. He had a catering business, and it was this that gave him the idea for supplying ice. In 1857 his first cargo of ice – 400 tons of it – arrived from Norway. It seems he already owned the building and had constructed the ice well in preparation. In 1863 things were going well enough that a second well was constructed. (The building didn't have any upper floors at the time – they were added in around 1904, along with the ramp that allowed the horses to 'go upstairs to bed' in their newly constructed stables.)

The building remained in the possession of United Carlo Gatti, Stevenson & Slaters until 1926. During World War II the building was used as a depot for spare parts for London buses. In 1956, further alterations took place, removing the stable partitions. The building was used as a warehouse by an Italian food importer, and then it was empty for some time before being taken over by the Canal Museum Trust in 1989. No structural alterations were made, except for opening up the hole in the floor to allow a view into the ice well. There are the remains of an Avery weighbridge in the entrance, possibly used to weigh the ice as it was delivered. The floors you see today were part of the 1904–06 alterations.

So why was the ice stored underground? Well, before freezers, it was the most effective way to keep it cool. An insulated underground chamber with good drainage could store ice for months, even years. You've probably seen ice houses at stately homes, usually out in the grounds, where they stored ice that was often taken from their own lake. Commercial ice wells in cities were quite common, although most of them have been filled in – these are the only ones you can look at in London, maybe in Europe – although a very large and impressive one with an egg-shaped brick cupola was found near Regent's Park as this book was being written.

The main demand for Gatti's ice would have come from the sellers of fish, meat and dairy produce – ordinary people didn't have ice at home, as it was too expensive, and there was nowhere to keep it where it wouldn't melt. The ice came to London by ship before travelling to Battlebridge Basin by horse-drawn barge. (The basin was constructed in about 1820 and was surrounded by industrial buildings – a flour mill, sawmills, a jam maker and a bottling plant.) Then it was transferred to the huge brick-lined wells, which are 30 feet in diameter and around 42 feet deep.

The wells were used to store natural ice until 1904. By then, advances in technology meant that ice could be made in London. The bottom pretty much dropped out of the natural ice trade business and the building was converted into a horse-and-cart depot.

You can peer down into one of the wells from the ground floor of the museum, and look at the other one virtually, using a webcam. You can also listen to a recording of the son of one of the men who worked in the ice wells, reminiscing about the stories his dad told him about what it was like.

While you're there, you should definitely have a look at the fascinating display about the history of ice cream. (To make ice cream, of course, you needed ice – that cream won't freeze itself.) It seems likely that the Chinese invented ice cream, using salt and ice, which react together to lower the temperature very rapidly and freeze liquids. A recognisable European version of the chilly treat was first recorded in Italy, and, in England, Charles II got to try some at a banquet in 1672. Mrs Mary Eales gave the first recipe in an English cookery book in 1718. She didn't suggest how you might make it smooth, though, so it would have been crunchy and full of ice crystals. It was, nonetheless, very definitely a luxury. As the 19th century progressed it became more common, with Italian immigrants bringing their expertise. Ice-cream makers used a box containing salt and ice that surrounded the container of cream and flavourings. The temperature drops and the mixture freezes. But to make sure it freezes evenly, you need to stir or rotate the mixture.

The Italian street sellers of ice cream were called hokey-pokey men – thought (perhaps) to be a corruption of the Italian for 'try a little'. As more ice was imported, the price came down, making ice cream more accessible. It was sold in little glasses known as 'licks' – which were returned, wiped clean (or not…) and reused. These were, unsurprisingly, not terribly hygienic, and were banned in 1926. Edible cones had already been invented, luckily.

Ice-cream manufacturer Walls began selling from bicycles and tricycles in around 1923, when they came up with the famous slogan 'Stop me and buy one'. After the war they sold 3,000 trikes and spent the money on… freezers.

....

canalmuseum.org.uk

12–13 New Wharf Road, London N1 9RT

t: 020 7713 0836

Open: Tue–Sun & bank holidays 10am–4.30pm; first Thu each month 10am–7.30pm

Adults – £5 / children – £2.50

Kelvedon Hatch
Secret Nuclear Bunker
Essex

If visiting a nuclear bunker seems like a strange thing to do on a day out, well, it is a bit. That's part of the fun, though – that and the whole 'secret' thing. Of course, it's not very secret now, with a website and tourist signs and advertising, but it's not that long ago that you'd have been able to pass by with no notion there was anything unexpected going on deep beneath your feet.

The entrance is disguised as a very 'normal' bungalow. The long corridor leads to a hill, within which the bunker was built. It's a bit spooky, to be honest – partly because you can't help thinking about what it was intended for. If you grew up during the Cold War, just the idea of this will give you the horrors, and the sound of the sirens is frankly ghastly.

Kelvedon Hatch makes a lot of the fact that it's 'the biggest and deepest Cold War bunker open to the public in the southeast of England', which suggests a number of things, including the idea that there may well be others – larger, deeper, and not open to the public. Who can say? There were at least 11 others like this one elsewhere in the country.

At any rate, it's an interesting place. If you're middle-aged or older, of course, the Cold War is your lived experience, and at one point the chances of you, a standard non-governmental bod, getting access to anything bomb-proof would have been pretty low. But now you pays your money and down you go, just as though you were someone important.

Built on land requisitioned from the farming family who bought it back when it was decommissioned in the early 1990s, the site began life as an RAF ROTOR station and spent a brief period in the 1960s as a civil defence centre. Then it was a regional government headquarters, designed for up to 600 military and civilian personnel, possibly even the prime minister, their collective task being to organise the survival of the population (such as might remain) in the aftermath of a nuclear war.

The tour is self-guided by personal handsets which are excellent and informative. There's an adult and child tour available, but both follow the same route. There are films to watch as you go round, giving further information, and a dressing-up area where you can try on various uniforms.

You can see the room where the staff would have plotted where the bombs were falling and planned evacuations depending on whether there were 'ground blasts' – the most devastating, as they spray contaminated earth about the place – or 'air blasts'. They would also have tracked bomb

falls in mainland Europe and kept an eye on the weather –
a wind blowing radiation towards us being just as deadly as
a bomb. The blast doors weigh a ton and there's plenty of
utility grey/pale green paint to keep everyone calm. You'll
see the two sets of filters for the air coming into the bunker,
and a cooling system – the human body produces a kilowatt
of heat an hour, so with 600 bodies down here it would
have needed cooling rather than heating. Are you feeling
claustrophobic yet?

Further down on the central floor is where the
government department would have worked, in their
rooms full of maps, computers and stationery, obedient
to the commissioner, who would have been in charge. In
another room you'll see where the representatives of the
various ministries would have worked, allocating resources
(if there were any resources) to survivors (if there were any
survivors). On the one hand, it's almost comforting to see
that someone – or rather, lots of people – had a plan, or a
number of plans, and that the results of a nuclear strike had
been considered to this level of detail. On the other hand,
you may wonder how futile this may in fact have been, and
what, in reality, would have happened down here with all
these people locked in together and only three months'
supply of food… How you feel about it probably depends
on your view of human nature. Seeing the inability of those
in charge to organise anything much these days, though, it's
quite impressive. No one waited until the bombs dropped
before digging the bunker, after all. They considered what
might happen and they arranged for the building and the
water supply and the refrigeration units, to say nothing of
all the office furniture and the living quarters and the spare
bunk beds in the tunnel, to help accommodate some of the

hundreds of civilian and military personnel who would be stationed here if everything went pear-shaped.

As the Cold War warmed up following the collapse of the Soviet Union, the bunker and its ancillary systems were unexpectedly surplus to requirements, while still costing up to £3 million a year. Time to give it all up and flog the site back to the farmer.

The tour takes about an hour and a half, more if you stop to watch all the films and take some time out to try on the uniforms. You might even have to come back another time to see everything.

Also on-site there's a canteen, plus Rope Runners, a high ropes course – quite the contrast to life below ground, this gives you a chance to hurtle through the trees. They also organise 'Nuclear Races' over challenging cross-country and obstacle courses, if that sounds like your idea of fun.

....

secretnuclearbunker.com

Crown Buildings, Kelvedon Hall Lane, Kelvedon Hatch, Essex CM14 5TL

For sat nav use CM15 0LA, access via A128

e: mike@japarrish.com   t: 01277 364883

Open: Mar–Oct Mon–Fri 10am–4pm, Sat, Sun & bank holidays 10am–5pm; Nov–Feb Thu–Sun plus school holidays 10am–4pm (last entry usually 1 hour before closing)

Adults – £7.50 / children 5 to 16 – £5.50

Laurel and Hardy Museum
Cumbria

Laurel and Hardy seem so quintessentially American, don't they? Their films were a BBC2 staple in the 1970s and 1980s, already a mysterious black-and-white Hollywood world of long ago. Bearing this in mind, you might be surprised to discover that Stan Laurel was born in England.

For a long time it was believed that Stan (or Arthur Stanley Jefferson) was born in North Shields, where his family lived, but Bill Cubin discovered that he was actually born in Ulverston (which at the time was in Lancashire) at his grandparents' house in Foundry Cottages, now Argyll Street.

This museum, like many of the others in the book, is essentially the result of one person's interest in a subject. Bill's collection of scrapbooks and ephemera grew to fill a room in his house, occasionally shown to other Laurel and Hardy fans. Eventually it had an official opening – with *Hi-de-Hi!'s* Jeffrey Holland cutting the ribbon, which seems quite appropriate. An extension was added in 1992 after – and this is a curious thing – someone won a Dutch TV quiz show and donated their winnings. The extension was opened by Bella Emberg – again, most appropriate. Bill died in 1997, but the collection remained in the family, the museum being run first by his daughter, and then by his grandson, Mark.

In 2009 the museum moved to the ideal setting of Ulverston's old Roxy cinema, at the same time as the town got its Laurel and Hardy statue (don't forget to go and look at it while you're in town – it's in County Square, not far from the museum and outside the Coronation Hall, on the balcony of which Stan and Ollie made a public appearance in 1947). Commissioned and paid for by the Laurel and Hardy fan club, the Sons of the Desert, the statue also features Laughing Gravy, the dog who appears in some of the films.

The museum is packed with memorabilia – it's hard to imagine there's anything Laurel and Hardy-themed that they don't have an example of – from dolls and figurines (so many figurines...), to salt and pepper pots, and to bookends, and illustrated plates and glasses, and on and on. There's also an amazing collection of photographs and personal items, including costumes from the movies and even the bed Stan was born in – allegedly. Now that the museum is based in the old cinema you can watch films on the big screen as well – they show L&H classics on a loop, so chances are you might get to see your favourite.

It is a bit tired in places – don't expect modern displays, or anything more interactive than one of those carnival cut-out paintings with a hole to put your head through. It can be quite cold in the winter as well – make sure you wear your coat. Despite these quibbles, you certainly won't find a more comprehensive collection of Stan and Ollie-alia anywhere in the UK, or a more enthusiastic team. They plan to continue improving the museum as funds allow, and there is hope that the release, in January 2018, of the biopic *Stan & Ollie*, starring Steve Coogan as Stan, will lead to an increased interest in the comic duo and further donations.

....

laurel-and-hardy.co.uk
The Roxy, Brogden Street, Ulverston, Cumbria LA12 7AH
e: laurelandhardymuseum@gmail.com   t: 01229 582292
Open: Easter–Oct daily 10am–5pm; Nov–Easter closed Mon & Wed
Adults – £5 / children – £2.50

London Sewing Machine Museum

London

This is another place that has limited opening hours, so make sure you check before making a trip to see it. The museum is upstairs at the Wimbledon Sewing Machine Co. Ltd, and it's not entirely obvious – it doesn't really look like the sort of place where you'd find a museum.

You might think you've come to the wrong place. But you haven't, so persevere. And don't forget to pop into the shop afterwards for all your haberdashery and home-sewing requirements.

Your first thought on hearing about a museum dedicated to sewing machines might be 'That doesn't sound very interesting…', but you'd be wrong. Sewing machines are pretty amazing, really. Just think of the enormous difference they made to life. It's almost impossible to imagine a world without them. If you had to make all your clothes by hand

and sew them with needle and thread, well, you'd probably have only one outfit. The technology seems very simple – simple but clever – but don't pretend you could have come up with it.

The collection is the personal mission, and pride and joy, of the company's managing director, Ray Rushton, who's been collecting for more than 50 years. He has more than 600 machines, some of which are extremely rare, and this is considered one of the most comprehensive museums of its type in the world. It has the very first Singer machine, and almost all of the collection is in working order – sewing machines are very robust, and their simplicity makes them relatively easy to maintain.

The museum is divided between two collections: domestic machines from 1829–85 and industrial machines from 1850–1950. There really is something wonderfully pleasing about the repetition of a good collection, and early sewing machines, with their shining wooden parts, engraved panels and beautiful paintings of flowers and foliage on a dark background, look fabulous. The wrought-iron treadles allow for flights of design fancy, and there are some great pieces of furniture as well – the standard sewing machine table (where the machine sits below the surface until required, when it rises up magnificently, like the birth of Aphrodite) is such a cunning and practical design. There are some really fantastically twiddly examples, as finely made as any contemporary piece of drawing-room furniture, with mirrors and drawers and revolving cupboards. The highly polished curved wooden cases of the portable machines are equally beautiful.

It's not just sewing machines, either – Singer, for example, made other haberdashery-related machinery, like the 'crimper' with heated plates that made pleats. There are overlockers for finishing hems, and specialist machines for sewing parachutes and corsets, or gloves, or for making button holes, and multi-needle examples for embroidery, as well as miniature or toy machines and more modern versions, some made by quite surprising companies like Flymo. (Flymo is a brand name of the Husqvarna Group, in fact, and they're rather better known as a sewing-machine manufacturer, although Husqvarna-branded sewing machines are now made by Viking. Look, maybe not every detail is interesting...)

The volunteer curator is very knowledgeable and will give an introductory talk/tour which is really useful, as there's not much in the way of signs or printed information. The building isn't very warm, either – well, it is a warehouse – so wear your coat if you come in the winter.

There's a good collection of advertising, posters and signs, as well as a shopfront. This is a reproduction and representation of the shop owned by Mr Rushton's father, which was not far away, on Merton Road. He began his business just after the end of World War II, fixing and restoring machines rescued from bomb-damaged homes. He didn't have a van, so he had to carry them – no mean feat, as sewing machines were, and are, solid, long-lasting pieces of kit and pretty heavy. As a child, Ray helped out, collecting machines on his bike. It was evidently more than a job to him, though, as his fascination has lasted a lifetime.

It's this fascination that led to him buying one of the most expensive machines in the collection, presented to Princess Victoria, Queen Victoria's eldest daughter, as a wedding gift. She married Frederick, Crown Prince of Prussia (the future Kaiser Frederick III), in 1858, and they had eight children. In 1886, the family's head nurse, Mrs Wakelin, left their employment and remarried – and they gave her the Princess's sewing machine as a present. Specially made for its first, royal owner, the silver-gilt finish is covered with ornamental engraving. It came with a cut-glass cover, complete with the royal coats of arms of both countries. The treadle is carved with imperial eagles and the stitch plate sports an engraved view of Windsor Castle. If that's not fancy enough for you, the instruction manual was bound in blue velvet with gilt-brass monograms, and there are ivory cotton reels with a crown motif. This historic and elaborate machine remained in Mrs Wakelin's family for many years until eventually it went to auction; it cost Ray £23,500 and became the second-most-expensive sewing machine ever bought.

The most expensive sewing machine ever bought is, naturally, also in Ray's collection. Dating from the 1830s, and still in working order, it is believed to be the fourth prototype by Barthélemy Thimonnier, who is generally known as the inventor of the sewing machine. Made of wood, it's basically one of the first sewing machines ever made. Thimonnier's work is very rare – and not for the usual reasons that things considered quotidian are sometimes neglected. His invention didn't go down very well with the women who did the sewing in Saint-Étienne, and they burned down his factory. He escaped, and went on to patent further improved machines, but they failed to make his fortune and he died in poverty. He'd be staggered to know how important his early machines are, how rare, and, indeed, how much Ray paid for this one – £50,000.

....

craftysewer.com/acatalog/London_Sewing_Machine_Museum.
html

308 Balham High Road, London SW17 7AA

e: wimbledonsewingmachinecoltd@btinternet.com
t: 020 8682 7916

Open: First Sat of the month, 2–5pm

Over-16s only – free (donations welcome)

Magic Circle Museum
London

The Magic Circle, established in 1905 by a group of 23 amateur and professional stage magicians, is a very discreet organisation, whose members are sworn to secrecy about the methods employed in their tricks.

As you might expect, you can't just rock up to their headquarters and expect to get in. Becoming a member of this very exclusive club is tough – although amateur magicians are as welcome as the pros, you have to apply, with your application supported by two people who are already members. Then you're interviewed about your interests, knowledge and skills. If you successfully get through that, it's audition time, when your technique, presentation and abilities will be judged. Then, and only then, will the ruling council of the Magic Circle decide whether to ratify your membership. It's not something to approach lightly.

If you *are* a member of the Magic Circle – firstly, how cool are you? – you (and your guests) get exclusive access every Monday for the club night (from 3pm). There are lectures and shows, and you can visit the museum and the library – strictly members-only. Membership is beyond the dreams of most of us, though, so what about your average person, interested in stage magic but unlikely to ever become a member? It's a secretive organisation, right, so you'll probably never have a chance to see inside? Well, luckily for you, that's not strictly the case. They put on lots of events for the public – check the website for details – and if you attend a Monday-morning 'History and Mystery' show (presented about five times a year), for example, or 'At Home with the Magic Circle' (Tuesday evenings, twice a month), you can have a look at the museum. Alternatively, you can book a guided tour.

Once you're through the front door, descend to the lower ground floor (the spiral staircase is very photogenic) and have a look at the wonderful collection of stage magic-related objects. They have some stunning theatrical ephemera, including beautiful posters for shows by people like David Devant (arguably the greatest stage magician of the 20th century, at least according to Jim Steinmeyer, whose eye-opening books about stage magic and the remarkable lives and personalities of late 19th- and early 20th-century magicians you should definitely read), as well as various objects and costumes used by famous magicians of the past in their performances, from Houdini's handcuffs and cabinet to Dynamo's trainers and Chung Ling Soo's elaborate robes. You'll also see a display featuring an original Harry Corbett Sooty – who was (is?) a magician, of course, and even had his own miniature 'sawing the lady in half' illusion.

The collection is fascinating, and also demonstrates the importance of the performer in 'selling' the act. Some of them don't look much – many are simple (or apparently simple) boxes and containers, like the cup-and-ball trick used by Prince Charles for his audition in 1975. (He made it through the process and has been a member of the Circle ever since.) You might know (or be able to work out) how some of the tricks are done, but still in the moment you'll believe the evidence of your eyes – however hard you try not to be fooled.

As part of your visit you might also get to see some very impressive close-up magic from a number of performers, and maybe some other things – a balloon modeller, origami, paper cutting, a flea circus... An entertaining and, dare we say it, magical experience is pretty much guaranteed.

....

themagiccircle.co.uk/visit

The Centre for the Magic Arts, 12 Stephenson Way, Euston, London NW1 2HD

Open: See website for events and prices

Mechanical Music Museum
Gloucestershire

Northleach is a pretty little Cotswold town with a huge and impressive church. It's also home to this charming little museum, full of the wonders of mechanical music.

As demonstrated by Brentford's Musical Museum (see page 162), there's something almost infinitely fascinating about the ways in which our ancestors accessed music in the days before radio or the internet. This is a much smaller, more domestic collection of automated instruments, but equally engaging. It's interesting enough for even the most casual visitor, but, if you're a fan, it's not to be missed. Take one of the tours and your knowledgeable and enthusiastic guide will lead you through the history of mechanical music, from music boxes to wax cylinder phonographs and classic wind-up gramophones. Anything that plays vinyl records uses pretty much the exact same technology more than a hundred years later.

Before regular radio broadcasts began in 1924, these machines were our only way of hearing recorded music, and they were proudly displayed in parlours and front rooms across the nation. The collection is maintained in excellent order, with an on-site workshop to make sure everything's in tip-top condition, lovingly polished and glowing with life.

There's a player piano with its covers off – allowing you to see the complexities of the mechanism, which is a sight to behold. You wouldn't think there'd be so much going on. In a cosy room like an Edwardian drawing room with William Morris wallpaper and the gaping, flower-like horns of various gramophones, you can hear famous composers like Gershwin and Rachmaninov giving concert performances of their own work via the magic of the reproducing or player pianos. They also have a number of phonographs and Polyphons – great gleaming wooden boxes covered in all kinds of high-Victorian carving, marquetry and twiddly bits, with a window that allows you to see the huge perforated steel discs that stand vertically within. It's these that play the tune.

If you've ever taken a music box apart – or one of those jewellery boxes with the ballerina – you'll know more or less how they work, with the barrel-like object covered in pin-like protrusions and the different lengths of metal that 'ping' against them as the barrel turns, playing the tunes. It's still quite impressive to see much larger examples, though, playing more complicated tunes. The Polyphon, invented in 1870, uses a similar method, with the tune punched out onto the disc and the projections engaging a ratchet-like wheel that plucks a tooth on the 'comb' to produce the note. They're powered by hand-wound clockwork motors.

There's also an absolutely huge state-of-the-art 1930s handmade EMG. gramophone, surely designed for loud, gin-swilling parties in a country house somewhere, full of people trying hard to forget the last war and hope there won't be another one. It may give you the urge to roll back the carpet and dance energetically.

The museum sometimes has temporary exhibits borrowed from other collections, or things that have come in to be restored, and they get a lot of repeat visitors, returning to see what's new.

If you own an antique music box that needs fixing (maybe because you took it apart to see how it works...) or any other musical item, there's a restoration specialist on hand who'll have a look at it for you and give you a free estimate for any work that needs doing. They'll also service it for you, and there can't be many places that can offer that. They sell restored pieces, too – but don't imagine for one moment that any of these stunningly beautiful machines will be cheap!

Guided tours last approximately an hour and run throughout the day, and there's a comfortable licensed cafe/bar.

....

mechanicalmusic.co.uk
Oak House, High Street, Northleach, Gloucestershire GL54 3ET
e: sales@mechanicalmusic.co.uk   t: 01451 860181
Open: Daily 10am–5pm (last tour 4pm)
Adults – £8 / children – £3.50

Morpeth Chantry Bagpipe Museum
Northumberland

Morpeth is a charming Northumbrian town and the Bagpipe Museum seems the perfect place to find here. It's housed (along with the Northern Poetry Library and the Tourist Information Centre) in the wonderful Grade I-listed 13th-century Chantry Chapel, built at the same time as the town's toll bridge (you can still see the remains of this in the river).

It was a grammar school in the 14th century and managed to retain its income during the Dissolution of the Monasteries. Edward VI granted it a charter and there was a school here until the mid-19th century. If you appreciate tiny details and delightful pride in place, the knowledge that the chantry also contains 'Morpeth's oldest window' can only bring joy.

So that explains the building – but what about the pipes? Everyone's heard of bagpipes, but Northumbrian small pipes are a bit more niche. Before a visit to the museum you might not be able to tell them apart, but you don't blow into Northumbrian pipes – they're worked by bellows which you operate with your elbow, filling the bag that then feeds the chanter (which plays the tune) and the drones (which play the background). It looks quite complicated.

The museum is not large, but there are more than 120 sets of pipes on display, including a miniature set made for Queen Mary's dolls' house. Many are from the extensive collection of pipe enthusiast (and master clockmaker) William Alfred Cocks (1892–1971), one of the earliest members of the Northumbrian Pipers' Society. He also made pipes, and wrote a pretty definitive book on the subject. These days he's considered to have been a very significant figure in the revival of pipe making – something else you may not have even thought about before a visit.

The collection also includes a set of pipes said to have belonged to King Louis XIV of France, and pipes from the Jacobite Rising, as well as a large collection of bagpipe music, both in print and in manuscript, and Cocks's collection of photographs and press cuttings relating to bagpipes – many of these refer to the early years of the Northumbrian Pipers' Society.

The exhibits are engagingly presented – it has to be said that bagpipes at rest are a bit like ungainly spiders – but the different fabrics used for the bags, the decorations and the variety of wood and bone used for the drones and chanters are fascinating in their own right.

You can find out all about them here, and about similar instruments. It's quite surprising to learn that bagpipes are not just a British development, but can be found throughout Europe – and, indeed, the world. You can listen to lots of them, too, through headphones, and learn the difference between a rant and a reel.

They run all kinds of live music events, including 'Learn to Play in a Day' and 'Meet the Piper' sessions, and the shop sells sheet music if you're inspired.

....

museumsnorthumberland.org.uk/morpeth-chantry-bagpipe-museum

Bridge Street, Morpeth, Northumberland NE61 1PD

e: morpeth@museumsnorthumberland.org.uk   t: 01670 624490

Open: All year Mon–Sat 10am–5pm; summer Sun 11am–4pm; bank holidays 11am–4pm

Free

Museum of Brands

London

Brands are everywhere in the modern world, to the extent that you probably barely register some of them. Brand names fill our lives, with some, like Hoover and Google, losing their capital letter as they become 'the word for the thing'.

Companies don't really like it when that happens – some even employ people to tell journalists not to use their name generically. A thankless task, surely. When your name becomes generic, it certainly demonstrates something about your brand above your competitors.

Anyway, if you've ever wondered about the development of the brands you're so familiar with, or what happened to those you remember from your youth that appear to have unaccountably vanished, the Museum of Brands is the place to go. It's a wonderful exploration of social history, with more than 12,000 original items, most of them everyday products, collected over the last 50-odd years by consumer historian Robert Opie, whose career in market research gave him a particular interest in the promotion, advertisement and branding of consumer products. He held an exhibition of his collection at the V&A in 1975, and then decided to open a museum. This started life in Gloucester in 1984, but by the early 2000s it had moved to Notting Hill in London. Ten years later it had outgrown the building and moved again, to its current site, round the corner from Portobello Road.

Robert has always been particularly interested in the history of 'supermarket brands', the basis of our food cupboards and cleaning supplies, but he's also collected anything and everything that we 'consume', from magazines and newspapers to technology and fashion. And why has he done this? 'I was struck by the idea that I should save the packaging which would otherwise surely disappear forever. The collection offers evidence of a dynamic commercial system that delivers thousands of desirable items from all corners of the world, a feat arguably more complex than sending man to the Moon, but one still taken for granted.'

The museum is arranged as a 'time tunnel', allowing you to take a walk through your own history as much as that of the brands. It's arranged chronologically and by product type, which is very satisfying – all the 1950s washing-powder boxes together, all the 1970s cereal packets, or tea, or soap. You can see the progression of design and what the advertisers saw as important reflected in what is highlighted on the packaging and the way the products are presented to the consumer.

Many of the early products seem quite unsophisticated, although it's refreshing to see things that just 'do what it says on the tin' – itself a brand catchphrase these days, of course – showing the way in which your market position and the sort of things you sell have a profound impact on the way you try to sell them. (Just think about the wilful obscurity of perfume ads…) Once it was enough to offer 'cleaner clothes without toil or drudgery' – that's got to be a win, right? Now even washing powder makes slightly more sophisticated promises about white whites and the removal of stains and germs.

Lots of the products we buy are the same as we've been buying for more than a hundred years, but often the way we buy them has changed profoundly, from going to a shop where someone fetched the items for you, to supermarkets where you get them yourselves, to online shopping where you only have a tiny picture to help you choose – all of these changes have an impact on how brands present themselves. Other things that have affected the brands we know well are two World Wars and the changing role of women in society. Who has money, and who chooses what to buy, is something of immense importance to brands, who spend a lot of money on research telling them 'what the modern woman' (or whoever) is interested in, and then amending their offering to match. (Did you know that Flymo lawnmowers were blue originally? Then they did some market research and asked a bunch of ladies what colour they'd prefer and voila, the iconic orange livery.)

It's astonishing how evocative the typefaces and colourways of very ephemeral objects from childhood can be – in truth, it's the ephemeral nature that makes them so specific. You (probably) don't hoard cereal packets or plastic bags, and lots of the changes that brands and logos undergo can be quite subtle – you might not even realise they've changed until you are suddenly faced with an earlier version. You will be surrounded by other visitors gasping in recognition as you pass through the displays. If you've ever asked yourself a question like 'Did Mars bars once have paper wrappers?' or 'Talc used to come in tins, right?', you'll be thrilled to see you haven't imagined it. And you might find out what the 'PG' in PG Tips stands for – have you ever even wondered? We take a lot of things for granted when it comes to the names of things that are endlessly present in our lives.

Before the late 19th century, brands existed, obviously, and they packaged their goods and advertised them in newspapers and periodicals and on posters, but the 1880s onwards saw a massive increase in the concept of the consumer and brands' desire to communicate directly with them.

Some brands developed as a response to particular events or the availability of particular ingredients, and their branding and marketing may be considerably more arcane than you realise. Did you know, for example, that Bovril was named after Vril, the 'force more powerful than steam' that appears in the novel *The Coming Race* by Edward Bulwer-Lytton, published in 1871? It was quite fashionable, and a number of things were named after it, but only the beef extract remains. Things with 'vita' in their name are often from between the wars, so Ryvita, for example, was introduced in 1925.

You might wonder when they stopped claiming that Milky Way was 'the sweet you can eat between meals without ruining your appetite' or that a 'Mars a day helps you work, rest and play', and here you can trace the changes in advertising catchphrases as society has changed. This is particularly noticeable with anything 'unhealthy'. You might also be startled by how old some brands are

– Kit Kats date back to 1935, Rowntree's Fruit Pastilles to 1881, Dairy Milk to 1905. Perhaps because sweets are some of the first brands we become aware of as children, it seems impossible that our grandparents were eating the same things long before we were born.

Although many brands have been subsumed into others – Rowntree's into Nestlé, Cadbury into Kraft Foods (now Mondelēz International), for example – the power of the brand is such that the original name is still the one on the packet. The value of the brand, after all, is what the larger companies were buying.

As well as packaging, the museum also features period clothing, magazines, cameras, telephones and computers, plus collections of toys and games – many branded with well-known films and TV programmes – as well as 'white goods' like washing machines. There are also televisions and radios – brands in themselves, of course, but also purveyors of advertising about the other brands in your home. Television advertising is extremely powerful, cementing tunes and catchphrases into your life, even if you've never bought the product. You'll begin to notice the connections between apparently disparate social changes – convenience food, the working lives of women, the passing of the domestic servant, refrigeration and the proliferation of plastic packaging.

You can also see how brands take on new looks for significant national and international events – like 'Christmas spice' toilet bleach, or heavily branded items to commemorate royal weddings, the Olympics or a World Cup.

The museum shop is very much like the displays of the collection, giving you the opportunity to buy more things and add iconic branding to your home. There's also a wide range of workshops, talks and temporary exhibitions, plus a cafe and a subtropical garden.

....

museumofbrands.com
111–117 Lancaster Road, Notting Hill, London W11 1QT
e: info@museumofbrands.com   t: 020 7243 9610
Open: Mon–Sat 10am–6pm, Sun & bank holidays 11am–5pm
Adults – £9 / children – £5 / children under 7 – free

Mental Health Museum
West Yorkshire

Although this little museum is only open one day a week, by arrangement, if you're in the area, or interested in the subject, you should definitely make the effort to visit.

The history of mental healthcare and the treatment of mental illness is complex and often unsettling and there's plenty here that you may find disturbing. It might be nearly 30 years since the closure of most of Britain's asylums but that's not long really, and although modern mental health provisions are a very long way from perfect and people are often still restrained – sometimes with terrible results – this museum reminds us that it used to be a standard procedure.

There are a number of things in the collection that you'll only have read about or seen in films – the padded cell, for instance, which came from the West Riding Pauper Lunatic Asylum (and even the name tells you a lot about what was going on in society when it was built, in 1818).

The museum was originally housed at the Stanley Royd Hospital, which is what the WRPLA was later called, and was known as the Stephen Beaumont Museum of Mental Health. When Stanley Royd, which was the largest mental health provider in West Yorkshire for almost the whole of the 19th and 20th centuries, closed in 1995, the museum was moved to its present location, Fieldhead Hospital. With the continued pressure from austerity measures in the early 2010s, there was some debate as to the viability of the museum, but fortunately a budget was found to keep it open, with the vision that it could perhaps do more than just explore the straightforward history of a particular hospital. Although the WRPLA's archive of photographs and papers (the treatment record books are kept by the West Yorkshire Archive Service) are kept here, along with a scale model of the original building, the remit is wider.

The museum explores the medical profession's ongoing attempts to treat the mind, whether through medication and restraint, or using occupational therapies. The wide range of exhibits, including a huge mortuary table, which is pretty much the first thing you see when you arrive, are all intended to provoke discussion and debate about the whole area of mental health provision, from the lived experience of the asylum's patients to the research work carried out by the doctors who worked there, including post-mortem research, as they tried to work out exactly what was going on in the brains of the people suffering from the various conditions they were trying to cure or alleviate.

Alongside the more disturbing exhibits – like the chloroform, straitjacket and manacles – are other, more encouraging objects, including artworks made by patients as part of their treatment. There's also evidence of the music and theatrical productions in which both patients and staff took part. The treatment of mental health has always been subject to fashions, if you like, and often quite extreme changes, depending on the latest theories and research, and it's fascinating to see the way things have changed.

The museum is full of stories, and it's these that the staff are keen to share with their visitors. It's easy to shudder and look away, but that does a disservice to the patients who spent time in the asylum, and to the staff who looked after them, attempting to alleviate their distress and find out why, exactly, their conditions had developed. Giving a voice to those with mental health conditions, rather than speaking for them, is an ongoing challenge, and one the museum aims to rise to. The museum's desire to 'promote understanding, combat stigma and break down barriers to wellbeing' can only be applauded.

The museum is an affiliate of the Happy Museum scheme, funded by Arts Council England, which 'looks at how the museum sector can respond to the challenge of creating a more sustainable future'. As part of this, it aims to combat social inequality, prejudice and stigma and become a resource for the history of mental healthcare in the UK. It works with the local community to engage with the complex meanings of mental healthcare, whether the patient is shut away in a hospital or living in the community.

mentalhealthmuseum.co.uk

wakefieldasylum.co.uk/historyinyourhands

Fieldhead Hospital, Ouchthorpe Lane, Wakefield, West Yorkshire WF1 3SP

e: museum@swyt.nhs.uk   t: 01924 328654

Open: Fri by appointment only

Free (donations welcome)

Museum of Scottish Lighthouses

Fraserburgh

There's something about lighthouses, isn't there? They always seem rather charming and romantic, involved in adventures from the Famous Five onwards. Perhaps the isolation of many contributes to this, and the fact that they are usually located in beautiful positions.

They're the perfect example of 18th- and 19th-century ingenuity and the urge to improve life and reduce risk. If you are ever somewhere at night where you can see the flash of a lighthouse or lightship, it's a comforting feeing, even if there's no risk that you'll ever, personally, run aground in a storm.

Scotland's coast is a particularly tricky and complex one to navigate, which is why it has so many lighthouses, and why some of the earliest in Britain were built here. Fraserburgh in northeast Aberdeenshire is still a busy fishing port and was chosen as the location for the first lighthouse on the Scottish mainland, the Kinnaird Head Lighthouse, which dates from 1787, and is built rather unexpectedly on top of the tower house of Kinnaird Head Castle.

It doesn't look much like your idea of a lighthouse – no circular tower here. It's more like someone's taken the top of a lighthouse – so the important bit, with the light in – and jammed it on top of a traditional Scottish castle. Which is more or less what happened. The castle was built by the Frasers of Philorth in the 1500s, but by the 18th century no one wanted to live in such an old-fashioned building and they sold it to the Northern Lighthouse Board. The plan was to convert it into Scotland's first mainland lighthouse. The cottages alongside, built for the lighthouse keepers, are more standard, with their thick storm-proof walls and square flat-roofed appearance, glowing bright white on a fine day.

The Kinnaird Head Lighthouse was recognisable by its white flash every 15 seconds, reaching a nominal range of 25 nautical miles due to its hyper-radial lens. It was in continuous use until the job passed to a nearby automated light in the early 1990s – but it's still in perfect working order and very occasionally still lights the coast here.

The excellent museum is housed in a fine purpose-built building just down the hill, and this is where you can learn about the history of the Northern Lighthouse Board, as well as the engineers who built the lights and the keepers and their families who looked after them. (It was a big responsibility – you had to concentrate, so no reading or music!)

The museum's galleries tell the story of Scottish lighthouses in an effective and engaging fashion, cleverly using sound and lighting effects to tell a compelling tale. This story also reminds you that the iconic image of the lighthouse isn't really what the structure is all about – the way a lighthouse looks (and Kinnaird is a good example of this) is entirely secondary to its main, indeed only, purpose. It's there to house the light. The light needs to be high up so that ships can see it from a long way away. And that's why lighthouses so often fulfil that 'tall thin building a bit like a pepper pot' description.

There are loads of child-friendly activities, including a keeper's uniform to try on, and they have the largest collection of lighthouse lenses in the UK (an amazing sight). You can learn all about the different types of lens and the engineers who designed and built them. You can also find out about the Stevenson family, who were (and indeed are) basically synonymous with lighthouses, building 93 over 150 years. When Kinnaird started to suffer from structural problems, it was Robert Louis Stevenson they called in to sort out the foundations, fix the walls and build the spiral staircase up through the middle of the castle. He finished the work in 1824.

At first, lighthouses were privately owned and built, which didn't always lead to efficiency and certainly didn't ensure that all the most dangerous areas were covered. After a series of terrible and destructive storms in 1782, it was decided that 'something must be done'. In June 1786, parliament enacted 'An Act for erecting lighthouses in the northern parts of Great Britain'. This act established the Northern Lighthouse Trust, which later became the

Northern Lighthouse Board, which still looks after Scotland's lighthouses today. They commissioned Edinburgh engineer Thomas Smith to get cracking and build four lights as soon as possible. Smith was Robert Stevenson's stepfather – and the rest, as they say, is history. The family's involvement in the construction of Scotland's lighthouses continued until 1938. The desire to get the light up and working as fast as possible explains why they chose to build the first one on top of an existing structure.

Once you've explored the museum and learned all about the lights, you can take a tour up to the lighthouse itself. You can see the automatic light that replaced it and the foghorn, too, last used in 1987. You can see the engine house that provided the power to the foghorn, and visit the keepers' cottages with their retro furniture and fittings, left pretty much as they were when the last keepers left in the 1990s. Have a look at the castle, where, as well as the tower itself, you can still see original features including the 16th-century kitchens and parts of the great hall, and then, finally, make the 72-step climb up to the light itself. The museum alone would be well worth the visit, but being able to see inside the lighthouse really does make this a special and memorable day out.

The museum cafe has splendid sea views, and there's a great shop with plenty of lighthouse-themed stuff to buy and a good range of books about lighthouses and Scottish seafaring in general.

lighthousemuseum.org.uk

Kinnaird Head, Stevenson Road, Fraserburgh,
Scotland AB43 9DU

e: manager@lighthousemuseum.org.uk   t: 01346 511022

Open: Nov–end Mar Wed–Sun 10am–4.30pm
(tours leave 11am, 1pm, 2pm, 3pm); 25 Mar–Oct daily 10am–5pm
(tours leave 11am, 1pm, 2pm, 3pm, 4pm)

Adults – £8.80 / children 5 to 16 – £3.85 /
children under 5 – free

Museum of Witchcraft and Magic

Cornwall

The Museum of Witchcraft and Magic is perhaps one of the best-known museums in the book. It doesn't always make it onto lists of the quirky or unusual, though, probably because these days it's quite a serious (though friendly and good-humoured) and well-respected place.

Since it was established in the 1960s, magical practice in the UK has moved from being a very niche interest indeed to something approaching mainstream, and certainly a fascination with the esoteric and mysterious is no longer seen as quite so eccentric. It's one of the most visited museums in Cornwall.

The museum's main aim is to respectfully explore British magical practice in all its diversity. It compares these practices with other belief systems, both ancient and modern. It's an atmospheric place, even more so when it opens in the evenings for candlelit visits. You don't have to book for these: just check when they're open and turn up between 8pm and 11pm (last entry 10.30pm). It's the same admission price as normal.

Although the museum has been in Boscastle since 1960, it didn't start life here. Founded by Cecil Williamson, who'd been fascinated by witchcraft and magic since he was a child, it was originally in Stratford-upon-Avon. The locals of the mid-20th-century Midlands weren't too keen, though, so he moved his collection to the Isle of Man, opening the Folklore Centre of Superstition and Witchcraft in 1951. The centre even had a 'resident witch', Gerald Gardner, who was the founder of modern Wicca. Perhaps not unexpectedly, this didn't work out long term, and Williamson returned to the mainland to set up a succession of witchcraft museums. Eventually, he settled in Boscastle and opened the Museum of Witchcraft in 1960. He chose the location at least in part because of the prehistoric evidence that 'from ancient times man and his magic making with the world of spirit were active in this area', and because he felt that the area was particularly spiritual and close to 'other worlds' – in Cornwall, he felt, 'One is standing on the edge of the beyond.'

In 1996, Cecil sold the museum to Graham King,

and it continued to develop, with a growing international reputation. The collection was expanded and the displays were updated. On 16 August 2004, a devastating flood swept through Boscastle, but Graham was able to protect most of the museum's objects, and, in the aftermath, the museum reopened with new exhibition space. In 2013 the museum and its contents were passed to Simon Costin, director of the Museum of British Folklore, and in 2015, the museum was renamed the Museum of Witchcraft and Magic to better reflect its collections and interests.

Although it's not a large museum (the collection includes about 3,000 objects and 7,000 books), it's easy to spend a whole morning or afternoon here and still not feel like you've seen it all. It's atmospherically displayed and lit and absolutely packed with fascinating information. If you're someone who has to read all the labels and interpretive signs, you'll soon have jammed your brain with esoteric information. Although some exhibits may be a little disturbing, it's no more than you'd expect – after all, you're not at a museum of witchcraft and magic to be soothed. There are all the expected skulls, robes, chalices, swords and wands, as well as a wonderful display of herbs and magical ingredients.

The exhibits are laid out over two floors, and there's no fear you'll miss anything because your route is quite clearly defined, leading you through various themed sections. Start with the history of the museum itself and its founders, before exploring definitions of witchcraft in popular culture, art and literature. There's a rather grim section on the witch trials, which is a bit of a downer, but then you're onto herbs and healing, which are rather more positive. There's a charming wise woman's cottage room setting, full of fascinating things to look at, and then it's upstairs to learn more about comparative magical systems from around the world.

You then explore belief in charms and symbolism through time, including hares and other creatures with symbolic meaning, the Green Man, and horned gods and goddesses. There's some beautiful artwork as well as dozens of amazing and thought-provoking objects. The stairs back down have tarot displays and other fortune-telling and divination tools. There's a whole section on sea-related witchcraft, most appropriate for the location. A final display explores the modern tools of the craft as well as providing information about mystical groups of various kinds, including Freemasons and the Knights Templar.

It's all very thoughtfully presented and will appeal to anyone – whether you have a specific interest in aspects of the craft or are merely curious – and the shop is everything you could hope for, with a great selection of books as well as what they like to call their 'wonderful witch wares'. You certainly shouldn't visit Boscastle without making time to drop in, and it's definitely worth travelling to if you're elsewhere in Cornwall.

....

museumofwitchcraftandmagic.co.uk

The Harbour, Boscastle, Cornwall PL35 0HD

e: museumwitchcraft@AOL.com   t: 01840 250111

Open: Apr–Nov Mon–Sat 10.30am–6pm (last entry 5pm), Sun 11.30am–6pm (last entry 5pm)

Adults – £5 / children 6 to 15 – £4 / children under 6 – free

Museum on the Mound
Edinburgh

Money. You probably think about it quite a lot – is there enough, generally – but do you ever *really* think about it? It's kind of magical, isn't it? Especially 'paper money' – after all, a tenner is only worth a tenner because we all agree that it is. In reality, it's just a bit of paper. Or plastic.

Anyway, the money we use, even the physical stuff (rather than the strings of ones and zeros involved in cashless and online transactions), has an intrinsic worth that's much less than its perceived worth. That's quite strange, when you think about it. This is known as 'fiat money' – what it's worth has been agreed and is supported by the government, rather than by a big pile of actual gold held in a vault somewhere. The latter was how banknotes worked in the beginning. They were 'promissory' – in other words, they represented coin held by the bank, and that's where the 'I promise to pay the bearer on demand…' bit comes from. You could go in and ask for an actual pound's worth of gold. Most national currencies no longer work in this manner – it's all done by fiat.

But whose idea was all this? Where did the idea for money come from and why does it work? Well, a visit to the Museum on the Mound will answer some of these questions. And they've got one of those machines where you put a penny in, pay a pound, and turn a handle to squish your penny and emboss it with a choice of venue-relevant images. Maybe a bit more exciting than that – only a bit, mind – are the neatly stacked piles of Scottish £20 notes. There's £1 million, there before your very eyes. Even if you had £1 million, it's unlikely you'd get it out of the bank in one lump sum – or in twenties – so it's fair to say that this is not a sight you're ever going to see anywhere else, and there's no denying such a large amount of cash has a certain pull. Shame they're all stamped 'CANCELLED'.

Elsewhere, you'll find Scotland's oldest banknote – not that old in the history of banknotes, to be honest, as China, Rome and Carthage all used promissory notes 2,000 or so years ago. The Chinese carried on doing so, and the concept returned to Europe in the 13th century with travellers who'd visited the Far East.

The museum is smart, well designed and modern, and is located in the basement of the extremely splendid baroque revival head office of the Bank of Scotland, a building both imposing and historic. Inside, you can explore all facets of money and economics, as well as the history of the Bank of Scotland itself, which dates back to 1695. It's part of the Lloyds Banking Group now and they wanted to close the museum in 2017, but following a public outcry (hurrah!) it remains open for the 50,000 or so visitors a year who come here to gawp at the million quid and find out more about capitalism.

The development of banks and building societies in Britain is an interesting subject, and the concept of building societies is particularly inspiring. Developed in the 19th century to enable their members to buy houses – something they would never have been able to do as individuals, any more than most of us would be able to – and improve their living conditions, building societies are still a vital part of the domestic mortgage market today. Britain's reputation as a nation of homeowners is certainly largely down to the concept of the building society. There's a section on life assurance, too – something else most of us take for granted these days – and you can apply for an 1820s-style life assurance policy. Will your 'risky' lifestyle increase your premiums?

You can see the large collection of coins as well as other objects that have been used as money over the years, including shells, tea and feathers, and admire the fine iron-bound 'kist' or chest (along with its giant key) that was used by the Bank of Scotland from 1701. In 1745, during the Rebellion, when the Jacobites were on the march, the chest was used to transfer the bank's valuables to the safety of Edinburgh Castle. You'll also find plenty to interest children who might not be quite so fascinated by ancient ledgers and so on. There are lots of fun interactive activities – you can even try your hand at safe-cracking, for example. Come on, you've always secretly thought you'd be great at it if you only had the opportunity – have a go here with no risk of arrest.

As well as the permanent displays, the museum has a special exhibition or event every summer and sometimes hosts temporary installations. Whatever's on, it's always free to visit.

....

museumonthemound.com
The Mound, Edinburgh, Scotland EH1 1YZ
e: info@museumonthemound.com   t: 0131 243 5464
Open: Tue–Fri 10am–5pm, Sat & Bank Holiday Mon 1–5pm
Free

Musical Museum
London

How did people listen to music before it was as endlessly available as it is now? Before the internet, before Spotify, the iPod, the stereo – the radio, even? Did everyone sit at home and play the piano, or sit by a bandstand, or sing to themselves? Or simply – oh, the horror! – never hear any music at all?

It depends how far you go back, of course, but let's just think about our great-great-grandparents here. There were popular songs, and sheet music was a massive industry in the 19th century. But what if you couldn't play (or sing)? The Musical Museum houses a collection of machines that would help you out. Some were intended for public use – they've got a fantastic art deco Wurlitzer theatre organ in their concert hall that lights up in a variety of incredibly stylish colours – but many others were meant to be used in the home.

A key thing about the museum is its staff. Mostly volunteers, they are the most enthusiastic and welcoming bunch, clearly all quite besotted with the instruments in their care. Visitors are fulsome in their praise for the team, and not surprisingly – the guided tours here are wonderful, and you should definitely make sure you time your visit so that you can join one. You'll learn all about the fascinating history of music reproduction, and being able to see many of the instruments in action is obviously a huge bonus.

Tours last about an hour, taking you on a chronological journey through the development of these automated instruments. You begin with music boxes and progress to the pianola played by Rachmaninov. There's recorded music, too, from the wide range of gramophones. Then it's off to the concert hall to see the Wurlitzer rise up out of the floor and listen to an engaging performance of well-known pieces. Once you've seen (and heard) all there is to see, you can check out the cafe, which has great views over the river.

The museum has perhaps always been a bit of a hidden gem. Founded by the late Frank Holland, the museum began as his own private collection – originally just (just! – there would still not be room for them in your average house) six reproducing pianos, which found a home in the former St George's church, Brentford, in 1963. This was supposed to be for two years, but 40 years later the museum was still there. It moved to its present, purpose-built home in June 2008 – with the set-up of the new galleries all done by the volunteers. Working here is clearly an absolute labour of love. The collection has continued to grow steadily over the years and is one of the most important of its kind in the world.

They have a state-of-the-art climate-controlled 'roll library' as well, home to more than 20,000 music rolls. A charming fact – when the museum first opened, a number of the actual pianists who had recorded these rolls in the early 20th century came along to hear them. Thinking about this makes you realise that, although the machines may be 'self-playing', what you actually hear in some cases has a proper human connection, just like any recording of an artist.

Apart from the music box, the self-playing piano is probably the best known of this type of instrument, but did you know that there are machines that play violins as well? They have one of these, a remarkable object with a lot going on – there's a piano, too, and it also plays percussion. As well as the instruments, they have various other music-related exhibits, including a special typewriter for musical notation, and the three galleries and concert hall provide an excellent, wide-ranging introduction to the subject. There's a good variety of interaction, making this a very popular outing for the whole family – your parents will feel nostalgic and your children will probably like all the noise. Make a note: there are special children's tours during the holidays.

....

musicalmuseum.co.uk
399 High Street, Brentford, London TW8 0DU
e: visit@musicalmuseum.co.uk   t: 020 8560 8108
Open: Tue & Fri–Sun 10.30am–5pm (last entry 4pm);
also open bank holidays

Guided tours & demonstrations: Tue 11am, 3pm; Fri–Sun 11am, 1pm, 3pm

Adults – £11 / children 5 to 16 – £5

National Cycle Museum
Powys

Bicycles are a pleasing thing to see a collection of. You have a firm idea in your head of how they developed, from velocipede through penny farthing to fancy carbon fibre-framed machines ridden by Lycra-clad folk forcing themselves up hills in the rain.

They've been at the forefront of the development of all sorts of things, socially: offering increased freedom, a practical reason for women to wear trousers (outrageous), and a way to escape the city for the fresh air of the countryside. The National Cycle Museum is home to more than 260 examples and aims to 'promote interest in all aspects' of cycling and its history.

It's housed in a fine Grade II*-listed art deco building, rather interesting in itself – it's an early example of a concrete- and steel-framed construction and extremely grand. Known as the Automobile Palace, it was built for Tom Norton Snr, who started selling bicycles in the late

19th century before moving on to cars and motorcycles. He was all about transport, even launching one of Wales' earliest public bus services. The museum opened in 1997 and was originally based on his son's (Tom Norton Jnr's) private collection, along with that of David Higman, the collection's curator from 1997 to 2010. In 1998, the cycles from the National Cycle Museum in Lincolnshire arrived, while Mr Norton's collection was returned to his family in 2014, so the collection has seen some changes.

As well as bikes, they have a really wonderful collection of advertising and ephemera – a large variety of tin signs for Raleigh, Singer, Michelin and Dunlop, etc., plus bicycling costumes (they have some fine tweedy bloomers). And, of course, they have some dioramas, always a highlight of any museum visit. These include an excellent mid-century camping display as well as wartime bike adventures. There are mock shops along a fake street and a variety of famous cycles (or cycles belonging to famous cyclists), including one of Chris Boardman's carbon Lotus bikes and Bruce Bursford's record-breaking *Ultimate*.

For a bit of interactivity, you can have a go at changing gear on a Vittoria Margherita, where you have to pedal backwards – this was an improved system when introduced in the 1930s, when most gear-changing systems were either very tedious (you might have to remove and replace the rear wheel) or very fragile. The Vittoria was much more robust, which was an advantage on bad roads.

The early bikes on display all have solid tyres, as the pneumatic rubber tyre developed by John Boyd Dunlop didn't arrive until 1887. It's amazing to think that people still went cycling even though it must have been incredibly uncomfortable. Once the inflatable tyre arrived, however, it made a huge difference, not only to the smoothness and comfort of the ride, but also to the speeds achievable by the cyclist and the terrain you could take your bike onto – resulting eventually in racing and mountain bikes.

The German Laufmaschine, called a 'hobby horse' in English, was the first machine with all three of the main things that a bicycle needs: balance, steering and propulsion. It was patented in 1817 and the set-up, with two wheels in line, meant you had to balance as well as steer. It didn't have pedals – you pushed it along with your feet. Rather astonishingly, no one developed this idea further until the 1860s, when the Parisian Michaux family, who made carriage components, attached cranks and pedals to the front wheel. This was the velocipede and it took the world by storm, becoming hugely popular in both Europe and the US. The main disadvantage was that low gearing meant the wheel went round only once each time you pedalled. Making the wheel larger to improve this wasn't very successful, as they were made of wood with a metal rim (like carriage wheels) and as you made them bigger, they got heavier, or weaker, depending

on how you did it. As a result, they weren't very sturdy and frequently broke, so they are extremely rare.

What was the next development? Spokes. It seems obvious, really, but a metal-rimmed wheel with spokes was lighter and stronger, so you could make it much, much bigger – only the length of your customer's legs would stop you – and thus the penny farthing appeared in the 1870s. Also known as the 'high ordinary', it was generally popular with active young men. They were happy to ride them long distances; remarkably, round-the-world rides even took place.

Further experiments in improved gearing continued apace in the 1880s, finally resulting in the 'safety bicycle'. This had a chain for the first time, linking the pedals to the rear wheel, and both wheels were more or less the same size. The bicycle as we know it had arrived. They had solid tyres until 1888, with the pneumatic tyre giving the final push to the machine's efficiency and popularity. There haven't been any enormous changes since, really – improved multi-gearing, lightweight frames and better suspension have all made things better for the rider, but your great-great-grandparents would have no trouble recognising (or riding) any of the bikes in your garage.

....

cyclemuseum.org.uk

The Automobile Palace, Temple Street, Llandrindod Wells, Powys, Wales LD1 5DL

e: curator@cyclemuseum.org.uk   t: 01597 825531

Open: Tue 10am–5.30pm, Wed & Fri 10am–4pm

Adults – £5

Children 4 to 16 – £2

Natural History Museum at Tring

Hertfordshire

If you mention 'weird museums' to people, one of the responses is often 'Ooh! Have you seen the Mexican Fleas at Tring?' and your response, obviously, ought to be 'yes'. It's more likely to be 'Er, not yet...' or 'What makes them Mexican?' Well, for the answers to those questions, read on.

The Natural History Museum at Tring is an outpost of the rather more famous Natural History Museum in South Kensington and was purpose-built in 1889 to house Walter Rothschild's impressive zoological collections. It's generally considered to be one of the world's finest collections of taxidermied animals, mostly acquired in the 19th century. Rothschild was both rich and eccentric, and from the age of seven was determined to 'make a museum'. His fascination with natural history meant he already had quite an assortment of butterflies, birds, mammals, fish and beetles by the time he was 10. The money to build the museum was a 21st birthday present from his father (it's all right for some, eh?). It opened to the public in 1892, and was gifted to the nation on Walter's death in 1937.

It remains one of the largest private natural history collections ever assembled. Dozens of collectors were employed to travel the world and bring back new specimens, as well as live animals which were bred and studied.

Today the building is full of original Victorian features, including the impressive floor-to-ceiling, glass-fronted cases, and the displays are arranged as they were in Walter's time.

So – what have they got? The collection of zebras is impressive, and you'll also see a polar bear, mandrills and other primates, extinct species including the South African quagga, and a collection of domestic dogs that, depending on your feelings about dogs, might make you feel rather melancholy. There's a huge ornithological collection, with birds from all over the world, as well as an elephant, a tiger shark, all the insects you could ever dream of, and the 'odd-hoofed mammals' including rhinos, tapirs, and various kinds of horse and zebra. (Rothschild loved zebras – you may have seen the famous photograph of his carriage, drawn by four of the stripy beasts.) There are a number of animals that were part of his live zoological collection, like the kangaroos and cassowaries, and there's a thylacine, the (almost definitely) extinct carnivorous marsupial known as the Tasmanian tiger. Marine mammals include a walrus and various seals and sealions, there's a Komodo dragon, plenty of snakes, crocodiles and alligators. They also have a glyptodon skeleton – glyptodons, extinct relations of the armadillo, lived in South America during the last Ice Age. They were huge, with a massive armoured carapace.

The Rothschild room explores Walter's life and enthusiasm for collecting, the history of the museum, and features a life-size replica of his giant tortoise. He used to ride on the real one, poor thing.

And what of the fleas? Well, there is a very large flea collection. Not usually something to boast about, but in this case it's a historically important entomological collection, with 260,000 specimens. If you have questions about flea types, this is a good place to start. (Amazingly, despite this enormous selection, they have examples of only 73 per cent of the 2,587 species and sub-species of fleas that have (so far) been described by science. It's still loads though, so don't worry.) The catalogue runs to seven volumes, and the fleas themselves are mostly slide-mounted. They come from all over the world and most of them are from the original Rothschild collection.

Then there are the fleas dressed as Mexicans, because why not? The story goes that when Rothschild bought these, he wasn't really aware of what he was getting – they're not a scientific collection, but instead represent a form of Mexican folk art, known as *Pulgas Vestidas* or Dressed Fleas. Around the turn of the 20th century it was a very popular tourist tradition. The fleas were dressed in their incredibly tiny outfits by Mexican women, sometimes as dancers and musicians, and sometimes as brides and grooms. Anyway, he kept them and they're on display for you to peer at through the magnifier.

The museum is very popular with families and can get pretty crowded – if you can, avoid during the school holidays for a calmer visit.

nhm.ac.uk/visit/tring.html

The Walter Rothschild Building, Akeman Street, Tring, Hertfordshire HP23 6AP

Open: Mon–Sat 10am–5pm, Sun 2–5pm Closed 24–26 December

Free

Newman Brothers Coffin Works

Birmingham

Now this is a properly unusual museum; you won't find anything quite like it anywhere else. The Newman Brothers factory made 'coffin furniture' – in other words, handles, plaques, crucifixes and all the other doo-dads that you might add to a coffin. The Victorians made funerals into a big business, so you won't be surprised to hear that all this began in the 19th century.

The museum is not purpose-built – it's the actual factory where these things were made. Costumed tour guides will take you round and explain all about the history of the company. You'll see the original stock, still on the shelves, the folded shrouds in the shroud department, and the tools and machinery used to make the fanciest fittings, which took pride of place on the coffins of all kinds of people, including Chamberlain, Churchill, and even the Queen Mother.

The Newman brothers themselves, Alfred and Edwin, were originally brass founders. They established the factory in 1882 and mostly made 'cabinet furniture' to begin with – hinges, keyplates and other ornaments for cabinetmakers to add to their pieces. In 1894 they moved to the current site and began to specialise in coffin furniture, and the company continued to work in this area until it ceased trading in 1998.

The production of coffin furniture wasn't much of a stretch from their previous business, using all the same skills and processes, but there was more money in it. The Newman family continued to have connections to the business until 1980, although their direct involvement ended with the death of Horace, Alfred's son, in 1952. The last owner of the company, Joyce Green, started out as an office secretary at the company in 1949 and worked her way up, taking over in 1989. She worked here for more than 50 years and it is through her efforts that the building and its unusual contents were saved for posterity.

The building appeared on the television show *Restoration*, which led to increased interest in the project and helped with raising the money required. By 2007, £1.5 million of funding was secured and the building had Grade II* listed status. Everything looked good, until – disaster! Funding was withdrawn in 2009 and the project had to be re-costed and plans revised. A successful bid for funding from the Heritage Lottery Fund saved the day and conservation work took place during 2013–14. The semi-derelict building was restored and transformed (as well as the museum, there are also units and work space for small businesses) despite plenty of challenges, with work going on even while behind-the-scenes tours took place. It may have taken 15 years but it's a tremendously successful and well-conceived project, and highly recommended. There's a short film, *The Making of the Coffin Works*, which you can watch on Vimeo if you want to see something of the scale of the task they took on.

One of the things that makes this such a special experience is that Newman Brothers basically didn't update their decor or office furniture or anything at all after the 1960s, so what you see is a proper time capsule. The 1960s saw the firm undergo a bit of a revival, and there's a tremendous archive from the period. It seems the perfect way to explore the history of the company, with the research and curation teams working hard to give a really accurate feeling for the atmosphere the workers would have experienced in their daily life. The shelves are full of unsold stock – stacks of boxes with their original contents. There are even old jars of coffee and boxes of floor cleaner, all of which were packed up and carefully stored until the restoration was complete, before being unpacked and replaced in their original homes.

This is a genuinely unique and internationally important collection, absolutely fascinating to behold. It's also a wonderful resource for anyone researching social history or Victorian funerals, or looking at factory work in the 20th century. It can tell us a lot about society's attitudes to death and expectations for what happens afterwards. The archive is so enormous that the research team has hardly even begun to look at it. It must be a dream job for anyone wanting to get their hands on a pristine collection that has barely had any interpretation. There are catalogues and order books and paperwork galore – and that's before you even look at the machinery, much of which is still in working order. You get to 'punch in' on arrival and some of the tour guides are ex-employees. There's not likely to be a better way of experiencing what working here might have been like. The museum does lots of work with local schools and volunteers, engaging widely on all sorts of topics.

You might think that a factory reliant on death might be grim or unsettling, but it's quite the opposite. The staff are welcoming and the atmosphere is upbeat. Death is inevitable, but it's certainly the case that many of the Newman Brothers' clients would have found the choosing of coffin furniture extremely comforting, ensuring that their relatives had a 'good send off' with everything of the best quality.

The change in tastes towards less expensive and more eco-friendly burials led, eventually, to the end of the line for Newman Brothers. Although this is sad in some ways – it's always a shame to see traditions falling out of favour and people losing their jobs – at the same time it's an opportunity for visitors to experience all this stuff in ways that would have been impossible before. (If it makes you think about your own funeral, make sure you make a note of your requirements. No one needs to be wondering what songs you'd want played as they deal with bereavement.)

The museum is always busy with events and exhibitions of various kinds, including Día de los Muertos parties, and a variety of talks and educational events exploring the changes in funereal traditions over the last 130 years.

coffinworks.org/newmanbros/visit

13–15 Fleet Street, Jewellery Quarter, Birmingham B3 1JP

e: newmanbrothers@coffinworks.org   t: 0121 233 4785

Open: Wed–Sun & bank holidays 10.45am–3pm; guided tours only, on the hour from 11am (tours limited to 15 people – reserve a place on 0121 233 4790 or by email)

Adults – £7 / children 5 to 16 – £4 / children under 5 – free

Jewellery Quarter Explorer Pass: This covers the Museum of the Jewellery Quarter, the Pen Museum (see page 184) and the Coffin Works. You pay full price for the first then get a discount on the other two, and it's valid for two days.

Old Operating Theatre Museum and Herb Garret

London

This place is brilliant, and you should make plans to go there immediately.

The area round London Bridge Tube station – Borough Market, Southwark Cathedral, the Shard, Guy's Hospital – is a fantastically rich area of London. Rich in terms of both cultural significance and historical relevance. It's always worth exploring, but you may easily have walked past St Thomas's tower, a square, red-brick campanile with a vaguely Italianate feel, without even noticing it's there. Step into the rather shady entrance and, beside the glass door of a dim sum restaurant, you'll spot a second, narrow doorway with an enticing blue sign: 'The Operating Theatre of Old St Thomas's Hospital. Please take care on the stairway.' This is good advice – the spiral staircase with its 52 creaking wooden steps is steep and narrow (there is a lift, but if you need it you should call in advance). It's

quite a strange contrast when you reach
the modern door at the top that
leads through to the shop (ideal
for all your medical-based gift
requirements). You pay your
money and step through the
shadowy doorway into a
narrow passage lined with
bottles. There's a faint hint of
herbs in the air, and a window
cut into the roof offering
a view of other rooftops.
Once this would have seemed
toweringly tall, of course, up
in the clouds, but these days it's
entirely dwarfed by the Shard
beyond it.

The roof space up here was
used for storing herbs for St
Thomas's hospital from 1702. An
area was partitioned off in 1821
when the operating theatre for
female patients was built.

As you come round the
corner from the passage into the larger space, you're
surrounded by endlessly fascinating objects, with
the working methods of apothecaries and chemists
arranged in a wonderfully organic and enticing fashion,
from ostrich eggs and stuffed alligators to puffer
fish, leeches, and jars of mysterious substances with
entrancing labels. You could spend hours and hours
up here, there's so much to look at. Polished glass and

wooden cabinets offer intriguing glimpses of pathology specimens, old-fashioned pill packets and terrifying instruments. More narrow, creaking steps take you up into the operating theatre itself, a reminder of why they're called 'theatres' as you look down at the wooden operating tables from the half-circle of the auditorium, iron banisters to lean on as you and your fellow medical students keep a close eye on the operation occurring below you. The fading light of a November afternoon falls cautiously from the rooflights, and a pair of gas lamps barely penetrates the gloom. It's a remarkable remnant from the early 19th century. A label on the floor informs you that, in 2008, sawdust removed from the floor of the theatre was sent for spectroscopic analysis and produced evidence of various herbs and compounds, including ether, clove oil and pepper, once used as a painkiller.

Once again you can read about anaesthesia – first used at St Thomas's in 1847, after a quarter of a century of surgery in the old operating theatre – and regard with horror the print of a writhing patient held down by six or so strapping assistants as the surgeons approach. The display of bone saws is not comforting. Even less so is the note informing you that none of the operations carried out here benefited in any way from antiseptic knowledge. 'Hands and surgical instruments were rarely washed before operations,' it says, soothingly, 'and bandages were often reused.' Patients often got through surgery successfully only to die from 'mysterious' infections. It wasn't until the 1860s, following Louis Pasteur's research, that anyone had any idea about germs. Joseph Lister developed an antiseptic carbolic spray in 1865, and reduced the mortality rate among his patients by a staggering 45.7%.

Back in the main room there are paediatric medicines like the deliciously named 'worm cake' – which was to stop you having worms, rather than being made from them. It was usually made of chocolate with a vermifuge to kill tapeworms and other intestinal creatures – which could rob a child of up to 10% of their nutritional intake, a real danger in those who were already malnourished.

The Cronenbergian display of shiny speculums and obstetric instruments such as forceps will have you hurrying onwards to less wince-inducing exhibits, like a selection of pestles and mortars. It was Josiah Wedgwood himself, apparently, who noticed that traditional metal mortars could contaminate the medicines made in them. His acid-proof biscuit porcelain prevented this, and similar vessels are still used today.

Dishes of frankincense and myrrh fill the air with exotic aromas. Both these resins had medicinal uses – frankincense was used against leprosy in China, while 10th-century Persian physician Avicenna recommended it for tumours, vomiting and dysentery. Myrrh is still used as an anti-microbial – an antiseptic – for strengthening the immune system and for fighting septicaemia. Other, more common, herbs and spices – such as marigold, cinnamon bark, elderflowers and lemongrass – are also among the ingredients laid out.

There's a whole section on blood-letting. You would think with no antiseptics, cutting people open, even if only a little bit, was a bad idea but it was a standard procedure for hundreds of years, believed to 'balance the humours'. They'd tie off your arm to get your vein good and plump and then open it with a lancet, taking just enough blood for you to briefly pass out. What fun! 'Cupping' was popular in the 19th century – the Prince Regent was a fan – and used a heated glass to create a vacuum over the cut, which drew more blood from the body. From 1821 onwards, more than a thousand people a year underwent cupping at St Thomas's – about a third of all their patients. (Cupping – without the bleeding – is undergoing something of a renaissance, with Gwyneth Paltrow among the celebrities photographed with the tell-tale blotches from cupping on her shoulders.) If you didn't fancy the lancet, there were always leeches – there are two very fine leech jars in the collection.

This is a captivating place, and you'll leave full of wonder at the curiosity and determination of doctors and scientists – and grateful, once again, that you live in a world where they actually wash their hands.

Note: Weekend talks (booking essential) are often held at the museum and are extremely popular. This may mean that the museum has to close due to limited capacity, so do be aware that 1.45–3.15pm on Saturdays and 11.45am–1.15pm on Sundays may be times to avoid.

....

oldoperatingtheatre.com
9a St Thomas Street, London SE1 9RY
e: info@oldoperatingtheatre.com   t: 020 7188 2679
Open: Mon 2–5pm, Tue–Sun 10.30am–5pm
Adults – £6.50 / children under 18 – £3.50

Pen Museum
Birmingham

They used to make pens in Birmingham. More than 75 per cent of the world's pens were once manufactured here. Nowadays it's hard to imagine, when you pretty much assume your bog-standard workaday pen has come from some immense factory in China, that the Midlands were where you'd find the heart of the 'steel pen' trade.

What would the world be like without the Industrial Revolution? Pens (or rather nibs – you might only buy a pen (or penholder) occasionally, but nibs much more regularly) are reasonably straightforward to mass produce, and more pens led to increased literacy – it's certainly easier to write when you have a standard pen that functions in a standard fashion.

Pens meant improved communication, too – think of the letters sent all over the world, buying things and selling things and describing places, people and animals that the letters' recipients had no idea even existed. And, on balance, this was a good thing – letters and articles expose bad deeds and celebrate good ones, as well as facilitating dubious practices.

The Jewellery Quarter has three great museums, so any visit to Birmingham really does demand you head over here to learn about the city generally and the specifics of the pen and coffin trades. The Pen Museum is housed in the Grade II* listed Argent Centre, which, among other things, was once home to the William Wiley pen factory – a stunning polychromatic brick building in the Florentine renaissance style, dating to 1863. (The Victorians certainly had no truck with the notion that factories should be dull or practical in appearance.) The building's design around a central courtyard allowed natural light to reach the workbenches from two sides.

Staff at the museum are volunteers and are very helpful and knowledgeable, and it's worth doing a tour if you have the time and inclination. A visit begins in the main exhibition area, where well-designed, informative modern displays explain the history of the pen and the development of the manufacturing processes.

A chap called John Mitchell pioneered the mass production of steel pens (before this, the quill pen was the most common form of writing instrument). Mitchells was the first manufacturer to use machines to cut pen nibs, which made the whole process much faster. In 1828, Josiah Mason came up with an efficient slip-in nib that could be added to a pen holder, making things even cheaper and more accessible, and by the 1850s Birmingham was the centre of manufacturing for steel pens and steel nibs; more than half the steel-nib pens manufactured in the world were made in Birmingham, and the industry employed thousands of skilled craftspeople. Further developments eventually resulted in the fountain pen, which from around 1930 gradually replaced the steel nibs. Although fountain pens were also manufactured in the city, it was the beginning of the end of Birmingham's relationship with the world of pens.

Once you have a grasp of the history, you can move on to the 'Pen Room', where you'll find a number of working machines representing the set-up of a traditional pen factory. You can follow the process and (very exciting!) make your own nib using original machinery, from punching the flat nibs from a sheet of steel to embossing them with the manufacturer's logo and the nib size, before bending and finishing them. In the factory's heyday, most of the workers were women, and they produced thousands of pieces a day – how many do you think you could manage? There used to be an incredible 129 pen factories in the city, all full of people pressing and punching and embossing and packing, so no wonder most of the world's pens were made here. People writing letters in Boston or Sydney would buy boxes of nibs and read 'Birmingham' on the label – it's quite a thought, really.

Pens in large numbers make for rather pleasing displays – this has always been the case, as you can see from the advertising displays from the 19th and early 20th centuries, where pens and nibs form endlessly swirling rosettes, swags and other attractive arrangements. The museum has examples of nibs from each of the Birmingham factories, and there are also signs, posters and other ephemera, and some beautiful display cabinets, along with a great collection of cardboard nib boxes – it's always interesting to see something that was once ubiquitous but has vanished more or less entirely. The peripheral industries are interesting as well, of course: the pen makers needed cardboard manufacturers and box makers and printers, all useful sources of local employment, and all gone forever. You'll also see some more unusual items, such as stave nibs for writing musical notation, and all kinds of writing-related exhibits, including inkwells, escritoires, early typewriters and Braille machines, ink bottles, blotters and affiliated items of stationery, plus period retail packaging from all over the world. It's the most comprehensive collection of its kind in the country.

You can have a go at writing with various types of writing implement, from reed pens and feather quills to the steel pens made on the premises. If you think this is for you, they offer calligraphy classes on-site. There's a shop, too, full of lovely pen-related stuff, so you can treat yourself after your calligraphy lesson and buy all the necessary accoutrements. The museum also hosts workshops and talks on the history of the pen trade.

Don't forget: it's worth thinking about getting a two-day Jewellery Quarter Explorer Pass, which will entitle you to discounts if you visit all three museums – the Pen Museum, Museum of the Jewellery Quarter, and Newman Brothers Coffin Works (see page 174).

....

penmuseum.org.uk
Unit 3, The Argent Centre, 60 Frederick Street, Birmingham B1 3HS
e: enquiries@penmuseum.org.uk   t: 0121 236 9834
Open: Tue–Sat 11am–4pm, Sun 1–4pm (last entry 3.15pm)
Adults – £5 / children under 16 – free

Pollock's Toy Museum
London

Usually when you revisit somewhere you last went as a child you're destined to disappointment. Everything changes, doesn't it? And that isn't necessarily a bad thing; it's just the way things are. Certainly, the streets around Pollock's Toy Museum have seen plenty of changes since the collection moved here in 1969.

The museum itself, however, has definitely changed very little since at least the early 1980s. It's almost uncanny. Apart from the addition of a Buzz Lightyear and Woody on a shelf in one of the staircases, everything is exactly the same as always, from the steep stairs and creaking floorboards to the mysterious half-light and typewritten labels. There's nothing interactive or digital going on here. If you bring your own children, you may have to listen to their astonishment not only at the toys but also at the setting.

Pollock's is housed in two ancient townhouses in Whitfield Street. Enter through the front door of the shop to a room hung with toy theatres (the Pollock family were heavily involved in the printing and production of these cardboard wonders in the 19th century), their papery stages and curtains ascending through the dusty crepuscular shadows to the ceiling. On your left is the shop, full of toys, mostly old-fashioned, mostly of the 'pocket-money' variety. On your right, a closed door with a sign suggesting you open it and pass 'Through here for Fun'. Immediately through the door a staircase leads both up and down, lined with glass cabinets filled with toys. It's very quiet. The stairs are narrow. There are layers and layers of paint on the banisters, 200 years of domestic decoration. You're here not just for the toys but for the atmosphere. For anyone younger than late middle-age, the toys won't be inspiring nostalgia, or only in a tangential way – these toy trains and tinplate vehicles are the toys of your parents and grandparents, this rocking horse has not been ridden in two or three generations, these dolls are the lost companions of girls who were young before World War II.

There's something about the contrast between new toys and toys that have been played with, isn't there? That's part of what makes a toy museum hover on the cusp of joy and terror. These toys are worn and chipped and scratched, their colours muted, their boxes faded and softened. The tiny fingers that opened the dolls houses have grown bigger, coarser, arthritic. It's strangely melancholic to consider the excitement of a long-past Christmas morning, when people long dead watched fondly as this bear emerged from bright wrappings to spend a decade – or two, perhaps – in the bed of his owner, and then in their own children's, maybe, before eventually making his way to this glass-fronted cabinet.

On the second floor there's a narrow doorway up a short flight of steps that takes you through the wall and into the house next door. Here there's a room full of dolls; across the corridor, dolls houses and shops along with toy soldiers, teddy bears and farm animals. Down the stairs to a room of theatres, complete with photographs of the original Pollock's shop, bombed out during the war, and Mr Pollock himself.

Toy theatres are wonderful things, and it's a shame you can no longer buy these complex cardboard marvels, with their curtains and flies and play books with characters to cut out and Victorian plays to learn. Think of the hours and hours of entertainment provided – even more if you could afford only 'penny plain' versions rather than the extravagant 'twopence coloured' and you had to colour them yourself. Sunlight, diffused by muslin curtains, fills this first-floor room. Are those children's voices you can hear, or is it just your imagination? Time to move on, past brightly coloured papier-mâché masks and shadow puppets from Thailand, and down the stairs once more to find yourself back in the shop. The whole experience now feels faintly dreamlike. Perhaps it's time to go and find somewhere for a cup of tea.

The museum started life in 1956, in just one attic room above the toyshop, which at the time was in Covent Garden. It gradually filled further rooms until there was no more space, and eventually it moved to the current location in Scala Street. It was begun by Marguerite Fawdry, who wrote the detailed little history of Mr Pollock and the museum that you can still buy in the shop. The museum is currently run by her grandson, Eddy.

....

pollockstoys.com

1 Scala Street, London W1T 2HL

e: pollockstoymuseum@gmail.com   t: 020 7636 3452

Open: Mon–Sat 10am–5pm (last entry 4.30pm);
closed bank holidays

Adults – £7 / children – £4

Postal Museum
London

You might be wondering what to expect at the Postal Museum. It's relatively new (it opened in July 2017) and has won lots of awards. It's split across a road in two buildings close to Royal Mail's headquarters at Mount Pleasant.

On one side is the cafe, shop and the excellent main exhibition, which traces the development of the postal service. This is very engaging, complete with a beautiful shiny mail coach and various pillar boxes and telephone boxes, ideal for the nostalgic among us. It's been put together with a real eye for a stylish display. On their website they say: 'We are an ambitious, forward-thinking institution with an amazing story to tell' – and this is exactly the impression you'll get from a visit.

Although the Post Office as a professional organisation didn't exist until the mid-19th century, people (especially important people) have always needed to communicate across long distances, and the exhibits begin with an exploration of how this has worked over the last 500 or so years. Writing letters, they say, was the original 'social network'. This might be a bit of a stretch, but it's definitely been an essential part of life for hundreds of years, even if, before the introduction of stamps, it was too expensive for ordinary people to send anything longer than one sheet of notepaper. Everything, from the stories of life as a mail coach driver to the information about the steam packet ships that carried letters and parcels all over the world, is well presented and interesting. There's lots of interactivity, from a range of historic costumes to try on to the thrill of the pneumatic tube. Oh, and did you know pillar boxes were originally green?

The postal service traces its beginnings to Henry VIII, who instructed Sir Brian Tuke to establish a national postal network to serve his court. As Henry wasn't the sort of person you wanted to get on the wrong side of, it can be assumed that Tuke jumped to it. The public have been able to use the system (for a price) since 1635, and those famous initials, GPO (General Post Office) date back to Oliver Cromwell. However, there were no records for the organisation until the early 1800s, when an archive was established by Sir Francis Freeling, Secretary of the Post Office from 1797 until his death in 1836 (and with a handy background as a spy during the Napoleonic Wars – always useful when it comes to efficient admin). This was just in time for the passing of the first Public Record Office Act in 1838, after which time every government or civil service department had an archive and was prepared to be proud of it. By the 1890s there was an official record room in the GPO headquarters in St Martin's Le Grand, central London, where the archive of the institution could be studied.

Essentially, this was the beginning of the museum, although the public didn't have access to any of it until the National Postal Museum was opened in 1969. The museum was partly built to house Reginald Phillips' Victorian stamp collection, some of which you can see in the museum today. Eventually, in 1998, the GPO HQ was sold, and the museum had to close. Larger objects went into storage, and the various collections were moved between various organisations as the Royal Mail was privatised. An independent charity, the Postal Heritage Trust, was formed in 2004, and the collections transferred to its care. The newly designed museum opened in July 2017, with Mail Rail following in September.

Yes – Mail Rail. The entrance is on the other side of the road from the main museum, and if you're wondering whether to bother – there's an additional fee to ride the tiny train – then don't hesitate: it's completely fascinating and very well done. If you're worried that you might feel claustrophobic, it might be reassuring to know that, although the train itself is quite small, the Perspex roof stops it from feeling too cramped, and the tunnels themselves are mostly lit and not much smaller than the Tube. There is an excellent audiovisual presentation during the journey (including a lovely chat with one of the former engineers, as well as a decade-by-decade exploration of life underground and the challenges of World War II and changing technology) which will certainly distract you from any worries. It's great, partly because it feels almost secret – Mail Rail was never secret, obviously, but nonetheless, the idea of the millions of letters moving unseen beneath the London streets is a romantic and mysterious one. It's changed very little over the last 90-odd years and is a genuinely unique experience – a brilliant industrial solution for the problems caused by London's eternal traffic congestion.

Once you've ridden the train and been returned to the 'station' in the old engineering depot, there's a whole further exhibition dealing with Mail Rail itself and the people who worked on it, with lots of little locomotives from the entire history of the system (which began in 1927 – it was originally called the London Post Office Railway – and closed in 2003) and some great low-key 'recent history' in the shape of the lockers of the final crews who worked on the trains, still full of their uniforms and personal possessions, as well as the tools they used to keep the engines moving. If you like to admire old tobacco tins used as storage solutions for screws and nuts and bolts, you're in for a treat.

If you can't make it onto the train for the actual journey, there's a great film that gives you a real feel of the experience. There are yet more interactive activities – try sorting mail on a moving train, for example, and throw various switches to keep the network running. Any child (or adult) with an interest in trains, history or being underground will love it.

The cafe and shop (which sells lots of fun London-themed books and objects, as well as a good selection of books about the history of the Post Office), back over at the site of the main museum, are in a fab airy, glass-walled room, with a courtyard for sunny days.

postalmuseum.org
15–20 Phoenix Place, London WC1X 0DA
t: 0300 0300 700
Open: Daily 10am–5pm
Exhibitions only: adults – £11 / children – free
Exhibitions plus Mail Rail: adults – £17.05 / children – £10.45

Ragged School Museum

London

The Ragged School Museum is housed in a group of three former warehouse buildings beside the Regent's Canal. They were bought by Thomas Barnardo and once formed the largest 'ragged' or free schools in London.

Barnardo arrived in London from Dublin in 1866, with plans to train as a doctor and then become a missionary in China. He was horrified to discover the city was overcrowded and disease-ridden, and that life for the poorest was almost unbearable. There were no educational opportunities whatsoever for poor children and, once he'd watched a cholera epidemic kill 3,000 East Enders and leave thousands more destitute, he decided his missionary work could be undertaken without travelling halfway round the world.

In 1867 he opened his first 'ragged school', which offered a free basic education. In 1877, the Copperfield Road Free School opened and within a couple of years was catering for 370 pupils a day, and an incredible 2,500 for Sunday school every week. As well as their lessons, the children were also fed and supported in other ways. Tens of thousands of children were taught here over 31 years. Changes in the law led to more government schools, and Copperfield Road closed in 1908.

The buildings went through a variety of industrial uses until the early 1980s, when they were threatened with demolition. The Ragged School Museum Trust was set up by a group of local people and the museum opened in 1990 with the intention of exploring the history of the ragged schools and the social history of the Victorian East End. The main element of the museum is the authentic Victorian classroom, and every year around 16,000 children experience a lesson as it would have been taught more than 100 years ago, doubtless to the absolute horror of many of them.

An exhibition space in the entrance area explains the history of the building and the influence of Thomas Barnardo, as well as other important local characters and events – there's a model of the Bryant and May match factory, famous for the industrial action of the matchgirls' strike of 1888, and information about the Battle of Cable Street in 1936 and the 1943 Bethnal Green Tube disaster. All the staff are very knowledgeable and engaging, and there's plenty to learn.

You should aim to visit during one of their monthly 'open house' sessions, which is when you'll get the opportunity to attend a lesson in the Victorian classroom. It's one of the original classrooms, restored to appear as it was in the 1870s when Barnardo set up his first free school. The high-ceilinged, echoing room has everything you'd expect in the way of well-used desks, slate writing boards and chalks, blackboards, easels and dunce hats, and an aroma of old wood, dust and glue. The teacher, in full costume and total immersion in her role, is terrifying – nervous children may need to be reassured that this is make-believe. If you have bad memories of school, you may need to be reminded of this yourself.

The lessons last for 45 minutes and you should probably come early to book (you can't do this in advance – it's first come first served when you arrive) as there is only a certain number of desks, and they need a donation before the lesson begins so make sure you have some cash on you. Also, if access is an issue, be aware that the classroom is upstairs.

As well as the classroom, there's also a reconstructed domestic East End kitchen, arranged as it would have been in the year 1900, complete with utensils and artefacts and demonstrating what life would have been like in a simple, one-room home with no electricity or running water.

This is an incredibly popular destination for school trips, and it's open Monday to Friday during term time for school visits, so be aware that there might be lots of children when you visit! There are also free family craft activities on Wednesdays and Thursdays during the school holidays, and there's a cafe.

This is quite a short visit – especially if you don't go for a lesson (you really do need to go for a lesson!), but there are some nice canal walks, and Mile End park runs alongside the museum.

---

raggedschoolmuseum.org.uk

46–50 Copperfield Road, London E3 4RR

t: 020 8980 6405

Open: Wed & Thu 10am–5pm, first Sun of month 2–5pm
(check opening times before visiting)

Free

Teapot Island

Kent

Calling Teapot Island a 'museum' may be a bit of a misnomer, but it's certainly home to a huge collection of the eponymous item. They claim it's the biggest collection of teapots in England, and as there are more than 8,000 on display, it would be hard to argue with that.

The general reaction of most visitors seems to be surprise that something that sounds so simple can be quite so interesting, but if this book proves anything, surely it's the fascination of repetition. A collection of anything is appealing – the same thing over and over again in different forms and styles and materials. Teapots are particularly good for this because you really can make them look like anything you can possibly imagine, although how effective some of the more outré designs are at actually brewing and pouring tea is another matter.

(It's a misnomer to call it an 'island' as well – it's more of a peninsula, but it does sit beside the weir on the River Medway and there are some nice riverside walks.)

But let's not quibble about nomenclature. Sue Blazye, the owner, has been collecting since 1983. She used to hold the Guinness world record for the number of teapots owned, although apparently someone in China now has 30,000 of the things, which seems like too many, frankly. Are they all different? That's hard to believe. All the pots at Teapot Island are different. They're arranged by category, which is probably a good thing, otherwise looking at them would do your head in. So, celebrities over here, buildings over there... animals, birds, floral designs... The ones shaped like tables set for tea with miniature teapots on them are quite meta. There's a couple shaped like cabbages that are strangely pleasing. And the Dalek ones are good as well, but you'd never be able to pour from them.

The collection is mostly of novelty teapots, rather than historic or antique examples (although there are some reproductions of rare antique pots – look out for the Minton 'vulture and snake'), and there's no explanation of the development of the pot, or the social history of tea drinking in Britain, or anything like that. There are vintage pots – by the very nature of the age of the collection there would be some – and a range of sizes from tiny to enormous. The labels generally tell you who made the pots, and sometimes the year.

The largest pot is outside – a 3m-tall teapot/ wishing well combo. Cast in your money and make your wish; the money collected goes to the Kent Air Ambulance.

Someone's passion or obsession is always endearing, so while this might not be somewhere you'd travel a long distance for (unless you're equally mad about teapots), it's definitely worth stopping if you're in the area.

The collection is usefully housed in a cafe – there's been someone selling refreshments on the site since the 1950s, developing from a tin shack that sold bait for fishermen as well as tea. You'll need a cuppa after gazing at teapots for half an hour, so it's good to know that the excellent scones are baked on the premises and the jam's homemade. And it's licensed, too – in case your reaction is to need something stronger than tea.

There's a ceramics studio as well, where potter Gary Seymour designs and makes various things – teapots, obviously, but other stuff too. His archive of teapot designs can be seen in the collection.

If you fancy getting a bit more hands-on, paint-your-own pots activities are also available. Have a go at decorating your own mugs, teapots or figurines – they'll fire them for you on-site. And there are teapots to buy if you want to start your own collection – more than 2,000 can be found in the shop.

....

teapotisland.co.uk

Hampstead Lane, Yalding, Maidstone, Kent ME18 6HG

t: 01622 814541

Open: Jan–Feb & Nov–Dec Mon–Fri 10am–3pm, Sat & Sun 9am–4pm; Mar–Oct Mon–Fri 10am–4pm, Sat, Sun & bank holidays 9am–5pm

Adults – £2.50 / children – £1.50

Public parking in Lees car park – charges apply

Teddy Bears of Witney

Oxfordshire

This is a shop, first and foremost, but as happens more often than one might expect, having a shop dedicated to one thing – in this case teddy bears, obviously – can lead to a collection of stuff that's not for sale.

They've always sold second-hand bears as well as new ones, and that's how they come to have a museum. It seems surprising to find that they were the first shop to specialise in bears, but before that, if you wanted a bear, you went to a toyshop.

Since 1985, this rather charming 16th-century building of lovely Cotswold stone, with its symmetrical front and double bay windows, has been what the owners describe as a 'natural home' for bears.

The shop is crammed with bears and other animals, many made by famous manufacturers like Merrythought and Steiff, as well as all kinds of limited-edition soft toys and a really fascinating selection of ever-changing vintage bears. Be warned – these are mostly handmade, specialist bears, and as such they are pretty expensive, as you might expect. The staff are real enthusiasts, so if you are a bear collector or want to talk about teddy bears, you'll be very welcome.

The tiny museum is free to visit and is home to Aloysius, who must surely be one of the most famous teddy bears in the world, having starred with Anthony Andrews and Jeremy Irons in the 1981 Granada Television adaptation of *Brideshead Revisited*.

For more than 25 years Alfonzo was the star of the museum. He once belonged to a Russian princess (Princess Xenia – cousin of Tsar Nicholas II) and was, when bought in 1989, the most expensive bear ever sold at auction. He still features in the book they wrote about him, if you want to learn more about his life, but if you want to see him these days you'll have to go to Denmark, as he no longer lives in Witney.

Another museum inhabitant is Bristol, who after a long life of adventure (he arrived with his original owner in 1910) was lost at Bristol airport, then reunited with his owner before coming to live permanently in Witney. As with a number of the elderly museum bears, a limited-edition recreation was made, so if you've been saving up you could have your own version of this rather charming fellow, with his one button eye, partly detached left ear and the red felt showing through his much-loved nose. The recreated version comes with a 'lost property' label – oh, the humanity. Poor Bristol.

The Old Witney Favourites are popular bears (and an elephant) from the museum that have all been recreated and star in the shop's catalogue – so if you've ever seen them in there, the chance to see the originals is quite a thrill.

....

teddybears.co.uk/about-us

99 High Street, Witney, Oxfordshire OX28 6HY

e: bears@witneybears.co.uk   t: 01993 706616

Open: Mon–Fri 9.30am–5.30pm, Sat 9.30am–5pm, Sun by appointment

Free

Time Machine Museum
of Science Fiction
Herefordshire

You might expect a science fiction museum to be housed in a flashy state-of-the-art building in a cosmopolitan city, but not this one.

Bromyard is a small market town near the Herefordshire–Worcestershire border, and is inclined more towards half-timbering than expanses of steel and glass. Therefore the fact that the museum is found in a narrow-fronted shop with wonky beams and two bay windows, that was once a bakery, seems more appropriate. The windows may have been designed with the display of cottage loaves and buns in mind but are equally at home with a pair of cardboard cut-out Daleks standing guard in them. (There are real Daleks inside.)

Some of the exhibits are downstairs in the 'Creepy Dungeon' where the bread was baked, and it's certainly an atmospheric setting. If you have fond memories of being scared by Cybermen you may be able to recreate some of that feeling – and if that's not disconcerting enough, they've got a Weeping Angel, so don't blink! And so forth. Depending on your susceptibility, you might find it genuinely quite spooky as you tip-toe cautiously from one uneven-floored, shadowy cellar room to another.

They've got a K9! And you have to go through a TARDIS to get to the exhibition – and who isn't going to be thrilled by the prospect of opening that famous blue door?

The museum claims to have the largest collection of sci-fi props in the country, and as well as plenty to please the *Doctor Who* fans in your party, including costumes worn by various characters and a number of Doctors, there are also exhibits from *Star Wars* and *Red Dwarf*, as well as *Life on Mars* and *Torchwood*, plus a very large collection of Gerry Anderson memorabilia, and props from *Thunderbirds*, *Stingray* and *Captain Scarlet*.

There are displays of toys and merchandise as well, so you can bore your kids by saying 'I had one of those!' a million times and wishing you hadn't let your mum give your *Millennium Falcon* to the charity shop.

The collection is growing all the time, with recent acquisitions including costumes from David Tennant- and Matt Smith-era *Who*, plus a Mechonoid from William Hartnell's *The Chase* episode, and a full-size TARDIS used by Jon Pertwee and other Doctors. Owner Andy is, as you might expect, a proper enthusiast who takes great pride in his collection and is extremely knowledgeable about the shows featured. He's really delighted to share his museum with fans and happy to talk about the exhibits.

....

timemachineuk.com

12 The Square, Bromyard, Herefordshire HR7 4BP

e: info@timemachineuk.com   t: 01885 488329

Open: Apr–Sep Wed–Sun 10.30am–4.30pm; Oct–Mar Sat & Sun 10.30am–4pm; Bank Holiday Mon

Adults – £8 / children 5 to 16 – £6

Viktor Wynd Museum
of Curiosities
London

A brisk walk of 10 minutes from Bethnal Green Tube will bring you to a small black-and-white-painted shop front, with a neon 'Cocktails' sign and a display of skulls and bottles. A sign on the door states: 'This is not a brothel. There are no prostitutes at this address.'

Those of you versed in your 1990s artists and dandies will recognise it from the front door of the late Sebastian Horsley, whose sparkly red suit is one of the exhibits within.

Once inside, you'll find yourself in a long, narrow, atmospheric room, with a bar and banquette seating. They have gallery installations up here, so there will be art – in 2018, an exhibition of the work of Scottish artist and writer Alasdair Gray. Stuffed bats hang from the ceiling and there are a number of taxidermied beasts, including a 'unicorn' zebra and a variety of antelope. Buy your ticket at the bar – they'll offer you a drink, which you might want. The museum, or rather Wunderkabinett, is in the basement, and you must descend a tightly coiling spiral staircase. Although children are welcome (before 5pm), it is suggested you might want to check it out yourself before taking them.

And what should you expect? It's said the concept has 'no overreaching aim beyond the theft of its visitors' time', although it's also the owner's desire to 'present an incoherent vision of the world displayed through wonder' – which is, I'm sure you'll agree, an enticing prospect. It's claimed that there is no attempt to categorise the collection – in fact, the whole process of identifying, labelling and contextualising the exhibits that takes place in more mainstream museums is anathema to the founder, Viktor Wynd himself, who wishes merely to display everything that has caught his eye. The aim is perhaps to present something more like a child's collection, before specialisation rears its head and sends things off down a 'fossils only' or 'just vehicles' route. As such, in many ways it is a complete contrast to many of the very specific collections described in these pages. And yet it's driven by the same urge to collect, even if not to quantify that collection.

There are two rooms, divided variously by cabinets and cases filled with – well – curiosities. There's a faint aroma of dust and old fabric. Above you, a case in which taxidermy squirrels are playing cards. In front of you, some of Tessa Farmer's unsettling insect and skeletal humanoid installations. There's Horsley's sparkly suit and one of the nails from his crucifixion in the Philippines, along with a number of newspaper articles about him. A hippo's skull covered in gold leaf – the hippo one of those from the menagerie of Pablo Escobar, Colombian drug lord. A taxidermy hedgehog, pulp fiction from the 1950s, a case crammed with shells and bones and carved African images. A two-headed lamb. What's here in the dark? Use your phone as a torch and try not to jump at the goat-headed gentleman sitting in the darkness.

You're probably getting the feel for Mr Wynd's interests here. Sex and drugs and death, anything a little morbid or disquieting or just plain odd. As you walk round, peering into the display cases, this opinion won't change. Stuffed moles, an elephant's skull, a hanged man, a hanged man's erection, a rejection slip from Faber and Faber, a giant spider crab with a tiny dolls' house dinner party laid out on its carapace. Below that, the skeleton of an anteater. In the Lion Room there's a Fiji mermaid suspended from the ceiling, erotic prints around the walls and a human skeleton encased in the table. There are drawings and paintings by a wide range of artists, including Austin Osman Spare, Stephen Tennant, Leonora Carrington and Mervyn Peake.

You won't lack for objects to look at. And generally they're labelled – so for all the claims that Mr Wynd isn't interested in context, you may not be totally convinced. Labels are always good, anyway; it's useful to know what you're looking at, or what someone wants you to think you're looking at. The whole thing teeters slightly on that awkward ridge between 'endlessly fascinating' and 'a bit pretentious', as you might expect something of this nature to do when you find it in fashionable north London. The hope that it 'fills the vacuum between what the establishment elite believes is worthy of worship and what exists in the world' may be a claim that you, explorer of such elite sites as a museum of pens and another of sewing machines, may find a little grandiose. There are few museums today that contain only objects associated with the elite, after all, and if putting things in a museum makes them elite objects, that's a whole other issue, don't you think? In any event, perhaps it's better to enjoy the objects here in all their cluttered oddness, rather than seeing your visit as in some way socking it to 'the Man'.

So who, then, is Viktor Wynd? Well, he's an artist and collector with an entry on Wikipedia, but the photograph of him in the museum, taken in the early 1990s, that shows a young man at Père Lachaise cemetery in Paris and which is captioned 'when I was a teenager I liked to hang out in cemeteries and write poetry' probably tells you everything you need to know. (This is not a criticism, by the way – if you can't write poetry in cemeteries as a teenager, when can you? Shouldn't we all spend a bit more time doing this sort of thing?) As a child, he had 'an insatiable desire to possess things' and this has continued throughout his life. As you can see.

There are temporary exhibitions and a wide range of events, often featuring literary figures from the more Fortean/occult/surrealist end of the spectrum (a cursory glance at Mr Wynd's influences will find all the usual suspects). The Last Tuesday Society has a deliberately complex and literary background – a 'pataphysical organisation' founded by William James at Harvard in the 1870s and 'inherited by David Piper and Viktor Wynd' in 2006. Since then, they've put on a multitude of events, including literary salons, masquerade balls, seances and exhibitions. The bar upstairs serves an exhaustive selection of interesting-looking cocktails and specialises in absinthe. You can book taxidermy lessons through the website – although these are not held at the museum. You can also join Mr Wynd for a guided tour (usually the last Tuesday of the month, 6.30 sharp, a G&T included in the ticket price) where he'll tell you about how (and why) he collected various items.

....

thelasttuesdaysociety.org/museum-curiosities
11 Mare Street, London E8 4RP
e: info@thelasttuesdaysociety.org   t: 020 7998 3617
Open: Tue 3–11pm, Wed–Sat 12–11pm, Sun 12–10.30pm
Adults – £6 / children – £3 (children permitted only before 5pm)

Wimbledon Windmill Museum

London

There are other windmills you can visit, of course – that's not what's unusual about this one. It's the location that's unusual. Wimbledon still has its common, so it's not impossible to imagine it as a village, just quite difficult. But like all the villages around London that have been slowly sucked into the city, once it was a quiet, rural place, with fields and woods and streams and, yes, windmills.

This one has been open to the public for 40-odd years, although at first it was only one floor that was accessible. That all changed with a Heritage Lottery Fund grant in 1999 and now you can learn about milling generally on the ground floor and this specific windmill upstairs, as well as other methods of milling – and you can have a go yourself using the saddle stone and hand quern, so you'll soon see why using water or wind power to do this task was quite the improvement.

It's not open very often, so make sure you check before travelling. The displays and exhibits are extremely comprehensive and well presented – it's hard to imagine you'll leave without knowing pretty much everything there is to know about milling in general and this windmill in particular. There's a video to watch about English windmills and their construction, and a really quite impressive collection of tools belonging to a millwright, some dating back hundreds of years. Don't miss the model room, which has some fab exhibits – who doesn't like model buildings? These are mostly beautifully detailed representations of real mills, which demonstrate the way the technology developed – windmills are probably more complex than you might imagine. And you'll find out why water has always been a preferable way to power mills, even if watermills are not quite so iconic as windmills.

There's a great diorama of the building of the windmill; it was built from local trees – obvious really – using a pit saw (they always look so thrillingly dangerous, don't they, pit saws?).

The history of the mill is also a window on the social history of Wimbledon, from the demands of the populace for their own mill, even though there were several perfectly good ones in Wandsworth, to the attempts of the 5th Earl Spencer, Lord of the Manor, to enclose the common and build himself a fancy house on the site in 1864. There was a six-year court case but in the end the villagers won, although it turned out to be a bit of a pyrrhic victory.

The mill was built by Charles March, who was granted a 99-year lease on the land in 1816. The rather unusual shape and construction of the mill may be because he was a carpenter rather than a millwright. He followed a pattern much more common in Holland, and very unusual in Britain, known as a hollow-post mill.

In 1870, despite the success of the 1864 court case, the owners sold the mill, removing most of the machinery, and it was converted into living accommodation for six families. One room of the museum has been restored to give an idea of what it was like at the time. The mill continued to be used as accommodation, latterly for the Commons Rangers, and in 1975 the first floor was converted into a museum. The Heritage Lottery Fund grant meant the sails could be restored to working order and the museum was extended to the ground floor.

You can find out how the mill's millstones work and see the tools used to make them, and learn about the various other pieces of machinery, like sieving machines, that you'd find in the mill, and about how the technology of windmill sails developed. There are also displays of the different types of grain used for breadmaking and some unexpected Scouting memorabilia (Robert Baden-Powell wrote some of *Scouting for Boys* while staying here in 1908).

There's a shop, with a nice selection of books on mills and milling, Scouting, local history and, of course, Wombles, and outside there's some old farm machinery and various English and French millstones. It'll take you about an hour to see everything.

Wimbledon Windmill Museum

wimbledonwindmill.org.uk

Windmill Road, Wimbledon Common, London SW19 5NR

e: info@wimbledonwindmill.org.uk   t: 020 8947 2825

Open: Mar–Oct Sat 2–5pm, Sun & Bank Holiday Mon 11am–5pm

Free

Author's Acknowledgements

Many thanks to Donna Wood for asking me to write this book. I'd also like to thank Dave Evans for the splendid time we spent at the Old Operating Theatre Museum and Herb Garret and the British Optical Association Museum, and Gwen Guthrie-Jones who joined me for a fascinating afternoon at the Antique Breadboard Museum. Thanks to Katie McCallion, who told me about many teaching visits to the Ragged School Museum, L J Trafford for sharing her thoughts about the Derwent Pencil Museum, and Samantha Tudgay for telling me all about her visit to the Museum of Witchcraft and Magic. I am, of course, always and forever grateful to Ollie.

Jackie Bates

Picture Credits

All illustrations by May van Millingen

Front cover main image: Erin Babnik/Alamy Stock Photo

Smaller images (clockwise from left): Life on white/Alamy Stock Photo; Dorling Kindersley ltd/Alamy Stock Photo; Feng Yu/Alamy Stock Photo; David Benton/Alamy Stock Photo; David Franklin/Alamy Stock Photo; Tim Caddick/Alamy Stock Photo; michael gamble/Alamy Stock Photo; Anton Starikov/Alamy Stock Photo